MW01634084

POWER PLAYS

THOMAS L. QUICK

POWER PLAYS

A GUIDE TO MAXIMIZING PERFORMANCE AND SUCCESS IN BUSINESS

FRANKLIN WATTS
NEW YORK   LONDON   1985

Library of Congress Cataloging in Publication Data

Quick, Thomas L.
Power plays.

Includes index.
1. Organizational behavior.   2. Performance.
3. Success in business.   I. Title.
HD58.7.Q49   1985   650.1   84-29091
ISBN 0-531-09582-7

CONTENTS

POWER PLAYS

*To my sons Edward, Timothy,
Stephen, and Gerald*

1

THE POTENCY PRINCIPLE

Power.

If that word makes you uncomfortable, summons up great ambivalence, suggests something that is both desirable and fearsome, you are quite normal. Most people experience some conflict when they think about power. It can be seductive. It can be repulsive. It can be used, and, most certainly, it can be abused.

Power is the stuff of fantasies: to have the ability, the strength, the resources to achieve what others can only admire or envy; to get things done when others are flailing about in confusion. (There is something of Walter Mitty in most of us.) Think of your exhilaration when, because of your influential stature, people in meetings give you their attention the moment you begin to speak. Higher management automatically gives your ideas and proposals weighty consideration. Your subordinates enthusiastically commit themselves to fulfilling your goals because they know that you have the wherewithal to reward their performance. When a position of greater responsibility and prestige opens up, everyone takes for granted that you will be in the running for it.

Power can enable people to achieve, for themselves and for others, success, fortune, victory, the good life.

But if power is the stuff of fantasies, it is also the stuff of nightmares. In all likelihood, it is the negative side of power that holds the attention of most people, even morbidly so as in the continuing fascination with Hitler and Stalin. It is impossible to forget Lord Acton's admonition: Power corrupts, and absolute power corrupts absolutely. Because many people witness examples of the misuse of power more frequently than they experience the beneficial aspects of it, they fear, suspect, disdain, resent, and misunderstand it. People who grew up in the 1930s and 1940s went to the movies a lot, and they could hardly be blamed for wondering whether all politicians and business executives resembled movie actor Edward Arnold, whose characterizations were often those of the corpulent, greedy, unprincipled powerful person. We read "Dagwood" in the comics and saw what kind of a boss Dagwood Bumstead worked for. Mr. Dithers was a loudmouth and a bully, never missing an opportunity to beat up on poor Dagwood. (Dithers was also cowardly; his wife beat up on *him*.)

These stereotypes were perpetuated by the early business novels, which were populated by characters who started their careers by being ambitious and wound up being ruthlessly so, stealing power from wherever they found it and, like rogue elephants, trampling anyone and anything that got in their way. Television continues the tradition of presenting business executives in an unflattering light in order to add color and drama to the characters.

Even without the stereotypes presented in fiction, the movies, and television, most young people in any generation grow up distrusting power. From early childhood they are exposed to negative role models, starting with parents who, in a child's mind, are unreasonable, autocratic, mercurial, and arbitrary. School, with its rigid, stern, demanding teachers and principals, generally provides reinforcement of the notion that power is more often abused than not. And how many adolescents escape at least one brush with the police, who are not always known to enforce the law gently, especially when the suspected culprits are teenagers. Finally, for some of us there is the military experience and a tribe of sadistic first sergeants.

Thus, for most people, there is no shortage of role models of people exercising power in an "unjust" or at least heavy-handed manner. By the time most of us enter organizations to start our careers, sure enough, there are bosses garnering whatever authority they can and holding on to it jealously, supervisors whose management style is rooted in intimidation, co-workers who spread malicious gossip, put one another down, and stab each other in the back. There are also crippling, demoralizing, stupid, power struggles. One of the most disastrous I ever saw was in the early 1970s: the president of a large airline advised his four group vice presidents that when he became chairman of the board one of them would be selected to succeed him as president. The corporation became four armed camps, with employees in each group expected to do everything they could to help "their guy" and to undermine the chances of the three other competitors. The airline is still trying to recover from the polarization a decade later.

Many of the unpleasant machinations described above seemed to be legitimatized by Michael Korda's 1975 bestseller, *Power! How to Get It, How to Use It.* The publicity for the book suggested that if you read it and applied its techniques, you might wind up with "a better raise, a better job, and total control over yourself and everyone around you." Some of the techniques are openly manipulative, probably have only a short-term effect, and are practiced by unattractive people with whom most readers would have a tough time identifying. There is reason to believe that the book was written with the tongue firmly embedded in one cheek. But many people took the book seriously, no doubt hoping to learn how to manipulate people for their own ends, seeking confirmation that, if you want to get ahead in the world of business, you must join the power driven, power hungry, and power mad. They are the ones who dominate.

Given the foregoing, it is small wonder that many people regard power negatively, or at least cautiously. Frequently employees in organizations speak contemptuously of the politics and power struggles of others. *They* "wouldn't stoop to that sort of thing," although, of course, they have to admit that "you really can't hope to get ahead without doing it." These people, certainly the majority of those in the business world today, see themselves as being relatively powerless. The contempt they express usually covers up their confusion about power issues. They don't want to be powerless (in some cases they actually perceive themselves as victimized by others' power), yet they say they do not care to pursue power. It is probably more accurate to say that they don't know how to pursue it. Or they see the effort to build power as entailing risks that they are afraid to take: stirring up competition, being rejected, losing out.

Such employees have bought the propaganda that going after power is the endeavor of the daring and perhaps thick-skinned few, that in doing so you must be prepared to compromise your integrity and to manipulate and deceive others, that in general the pursuit of power stamps one as being not "nice."

In short, people who disdain power usually don't understand it, don't see themselves as having it, don't know how to go about getting it, and fear it in others. Their misunderstanding of power—and its legitimacy—robs them of achievement, and of satisfaction in their work and careers, and it contributes greatly to their frustrations and feelings of helplessness, of being controlled by events and others.

THE POSITIVE SIDE OF POWER

The thesis of this book is that anyone who works in any kind of organization can have power. Power is a very desirable thing to have, because power is simply the ability to get things done, to obtain results. The more powerful you are, the more you can hope to achieve. This reduces power to manageable and relevant proportions.

Power has no inherent moral value. Power is neither good nor bad in itself. Whether it can be said to be moral or immoral, ethical or unethical depends on the ends to which it is applied and the way it is applied. For example, Ted competes with Bill for a promotion. Ted wants to beat Bill, which is not a bad thing. But, if in order to weaken Bill's chances, Ted spreads scurrilous gossip about Bill, that is bad. Or if Ted wants not only to win the promotion, but, in doing so, to blunt Bill's career, actually to do him in, that is an unworthy objective.

It is important to emphasize the moral neutrality of power, especially in view of all the negative stereotyping that we see. The use of power to achieve the goals of the organization is not only acceptable but expected behavior. The same applies to the accomplishment of important objectives as long as they are consistent with the values and goals of the organization.

Power is especially important to managers and supervisors, who must depend on others to help them get the results for which they, the managers and supervisors, are responsible. To take this one step further, it is usually necessary for a manager or a supervisor to seek *more* power than his or her position grants. It is almost axiomatic that someone in a managerial position will have more responsibility than authority to meet that responsibility. This is because managers depend on people over whom they have no direct control. Whatever the manager's department produces—a product or a component of that product, a service or a program, other people are involved who do not work in that department. The editor of this book is a good example of someone whose responsibility can exceed his or her authority. This person is ultimately responsible for the publication, but must coordinate with the legal staff who draws up and approves contracts with authors, work with a production department that oversees the typesetting and printing, with a financial group that helps to establish a budget and a price for the book, and with marketing people who advertise, sell, and distribute the copies. The editor, even though primarily responsible for the finished product, does not have authority over these other work groups. If the book is not published on schedule, chances are that the editor will have to bear the blame no matter where delays might have occurred.

It is rare that a manager's authority will match his or her responsibility. One of the more extreme examples of disparity I have seen was an editor of a weekly newsletter. He depended on several other staff writers to contribute articles to the newsletter he edited, but he had absolutely no authority over them. They all reported to a common boss. Each week, therefore, he depended on persuasion, negotiation, good will, and their professionalism to put together a newsletter that went to tens of thousands of people. (As you'll see later in the book, persuasion and negotiation can be very effective in building and exercising power.)

Because of the inadequacy of formal authority, managers in an organization will supplement the formal structure with an informal one. Imagine two managers who must work together even though they are in different departments reporting to different bosses. Because of the different lines of authority, Manager A should communicate with Manager B through her boss, who would then talk to Manager B's boss. But since this process is cumbersome and time consuming, Managers A and B get together and work out a less formal way to cooperate and communicate. In fact, there may be much interaction between A and B that their respective bosses know little about.

Another common example of an informal structure is an unofficial reporting relationship that is created when the designated boss is not the functioning boss. Sam Ply has been in a corporation for many years. He is only two or three years away from retirement. He is ostensibly in charge of research and development, but he doesn't manage much because he likes to do his own tinkering and puttering. Sam's assistant knows that the person who is really in charge is the executive vice president. When the assistant needs advice, a decision, or approval he goes to the higher executive. Sam knows and tacitly agrees. Thus a power relationship grows that is not reflected on the organization chart.

The above two cases demonstrate the necessity for looking at the informal as well as the formal structure of an organization. That is the meaning of the expression, "If you want to know what is going on, you must study the white spaces between the boxes as well as the boxes themselves." There are vacuums there, and people will often move into them to increase their power and influence. Some people do it so aggressively and widely that they become known in the organization as empire builders. But a certain amount of expanding is desirable, even necessary, if you are to be effective, that is, if you are to get the results you want.

Power helps to control interactions with others.

Control has a negative connotation, but it needn't have. Control is different from domination. Control is guiding a transaction with one or more others toward a desired conclusion. Whether you seek a raise from your boss, cooperation with a colleague, better performance from a subordinate, you need to be in control of the process so that you are more likely to get what you want. It is much the same as a sales interview. A salesperson controls the interview. He or she knows the desired conclusion: your business. The salesperson doesn't force you to sign. Instead, he or she knows how to guide the transaction toward the act of signing. In almost every kind of interaction you have with another person, you want something to happen as a result, if only the increased good will of that other person. Power techniques will help you to achieve what you want.

Power enables you to develop more options, more choices for yourself, as you apply power techniques to gain control over more resources—people, equipment, money, information. For example, you are a national sales manager, supervising the field activities of a number of salespeople. As you acquire more power, you have the money and the personnel to experiment with new methods of selling that you have learned about, such as direct mail. You don't have to go to your boss and ask for the funds, you already have them in your budget. You don't have to get permission from higher management to negotiate with the data processing specialists to design the campaign, you've already established the relationship. You have more options, more choices, more ways to solve problems. Most people, by contrast, operate with limited options. When you build power for yourself, you become aware of how much more freedom you have: the more power, the more options, the more freedom.

In addition to exercising control over the interactions you have with others and the options you have for yourself, you will enjoy other benefits from building your power and influence:

More results from others. The more legitimately powerful you become, the greater motivation others will experience to work with you. In the first place, you're a winner, and people like to associate with someone who is effective, who can get the job done right. Secondly, your co-workers will perceive that they can increase their power by being associated with you, just as you have perhaps benefited by your association with another powerful person in the organization. Thirdly, people will be hesitant to turn down your requests or to fail you if you have the power to get back at them.

Control of your life. You know what you need and want, from your work, the organization, your career, and others. Knowing what you want and where you are going is an important early step in building your power base. You call the shots, increasingly so as you go up the power ladder. You do not sit by and wait for others to tell you what you must do, what you are permitted to do. You gradually acquire more control over your progress, your direction, and your objectives by eliminating the constraints that organization and authority have placed on you. The system is self-perpetuating: each time you get rid of a constraint, your increased power makes others more reluctant to try to constrain you.

Respect and admiration. Whether people like you for being powerful or not, they will respect you as long as your methods for building that power have been ethical and not manipulative, and as long as your power is truly substantial and not merely based on an impressive style. The more power you accumulate, the less likely it is that people will be fond of you. They may even fear you a bit. But, however ambivalent they may feel about power, they will admire you for having become as influential as you are.

Self-esteem. You have grown, pushed out your boundaries, taken risks, and assumed control of your life and career. You have every right to admire yourself, as long as you don't have to look back on a trail of broken bodies. If you have been forthright and honest about what you want, you will agree you're in good company with yourself. You're bound to be an interesting person.

How you can move to expand your influence, to increase your effectiveness, and to get the results you want more often by building your power base and establishing power relationships is the subject of this book. You will have to be able to recognize and combat undesired, perhaps even unethical efforts to influence you and exercise control over you, and this book should be able to help. But more importantly, you want power-building techniques that you can be comfortable with, that you can live with and will not regret. Thus, the techniques and approaches and behaviors in this book will conform to the following focus:

Authenticity. What you do, how you behave, should reflect you. While you don't need to reveal all of your objectives, agenda, and purposes to everyone with whom you deal, you must not act in a manner that deliberately deceives others as to what you are about. When you are authentic and genuine, you are reasonably congruent, psychologically speaking. That is, what you say and what you do reflect how you really feel and what you really are.

Long-term results. If you practice deception and chicanery, you will be unmasked, and you will gradually lose your power. As the old Chinese saying goes, "You fool me once, shame on you. You fool me twice, shame on me." There is no point in seeking short-range results at the expense of long-term credibility and influence. What you are undoubtedly looking for are steps that will help you have influence now over people and events and will help build a power base for the future. As you build your permanent power, you will find, as I have pointed out, that people will respect you more, thereby adding to the strength of your base.

Substance. Style is important. There are actions you can take, manners you can adopt, clothes you can wear, and speaking styles you can perfect that will project the message that you are influential. But if the power is not really there, you will eventually lose face and credibility. Your style must therefore be rooted in the real thing.

POLITICS? YES!

As much as employees complain about the prevalence of politics in their organizations, as much as they suggest that politics impede the progress of the organization, the fact is that politics can be a sign of vitality, that politics, far from being an impediment, promote the welfare of any organization. When people of varying backgrounds, preferences, prejudices, expertise, and perspectives come together in one enterprise, there are bound to be differences of opinions, priorities, and objectives. Each partisan is advancing those values that are important to him or her. That makes for a certain amount of strife. But if there were no competition of ideas, it would be a clear indication that nothing much was happening.

Similarly, when a number of people in the organization are trying to increase their power, there will be competition, and that can be healthy. Competition can encourage people to work harder, to invest themselves more efficiently, to try to win. As long as there is not widespread withholding of information and cooperation, frequent efforts to do others in, or vast barriers to communication, the organization stands to win along with some of the participants in the contest.

Yes, there are risks to expanding your power and promoting yourself. But the alternative is to abdicate at least a degree of control over your life and standing in the organization. You will expend so much effort warding off attempts by others to infringe on your territory that you won't have much left to advance your career. You will find yourself at the mercy of forces over which you cannot exercise control. This is a rather dismal way to spend your life.

Politics can be fun. So can power building. Remember the potency principle: Power equals control and effectiveness. Power enables you to run things for yourself, to get the results you want more often.

2

WINNERS
AND LOSERS

In every organization you can find people who seek power, sometimes in the face of adversity and at great odds, and you can also see those who, for some reason, have decided or learned to be powerless. Paul F. is a good example of someone who has abdicated responsibility and assumed a powerless role.

Paul is a district manager who heads an office in a medium-sized city on the Atlantic seaboard. There are approximately forty people who report to the six supervisors under Paul's management.

As you walk into the district office, the first thing you notice is that it is shabby. The paint is peeling and dirty. The linoleum on the floor is worn thin. Looking more closely you will see a layer of dust on windowsills, dirt in corners and on the stairs. Paper that has fallen out of overflowing wastebaskets lies on the floor. Clearly this office needs not only renovation but simple house-keeping.

The central air conditioner is broken. It has been broken for several weeks. Paul has been unable to get approval for the repair.

The delay in getting approval for the repair of the air conditioner is, according to Paul, typical. To date, more than a third of the people working in the main room do not have telephones at their desks. The home office keeps promising that the phone situation will be corrected shortly. Paul has asked that the walls be painted, but he gets the response that it must await next year's budget.

Morale, Paul says, is very low. To begin with, he explains, his people are overworked. He has not been able to get replacements for those of his staff who have transferred, resigned, or retired. Another reason for the demoralization is the conduct of the home office. People there will call members of his staff asking for information "immediately if not sooner," and disrupting their schedules. These requests are not coordinated and sometimes duplicate or overlap one another. It is therefore almost impossible for his people to plan their time effectively. They are usually behind, and that creates much friction between the district office and the home office.

Some people in the office have to work harder than others who just refuse to accept their share of the burden. There are three or four whom Paul talks about firing. But Paul has decided it isn't worth the time, pain, and effort.

Morale is low, and so is motivation. But there's nothing that can be done. Working conditions are bad;

they impede productivity. But nothing can be done about them either. Yet, Paul is reminded that another district manager has been successful in getting allocations for equipment and remodeling. His response: "Yes, but he knows the right people."

Paul is helpless. There is nothing he can do about anything. Whatever suggestions are made to him, whatever examples of managers in his category who have taken action successfully against the problems he faces, his response is almost invariably, "Yes, but . . ." Paul is a victim of the system. Other managers might resist victimization, might prevail over it. But Paul can't. He will have a ready reason, a rationalization, for why other people have power and he does not. Paul's management style is "management by martyrdom." A martyr awaits his or her fate. As a martyr, the person cannot resist the unpleasant things that are happening. It is the martyr's fate to suffer. There may be grace in the martyr manager's suffering, but there is not much consolation for his or her employees. They need help. They need direction. They need someone who will take charge, who will intercede on their behalf.

Although Paul would disagree, there are some practical steps he has the power to take as district manager:

1. He could insist on normal housekeeping. Other district offices we visited, even though shabby, were clean. There was no dust in the corners, there were no papers on the floor. Files on desks were kept neat. The manager who permits poor housekeeping risks broadcasting a message of not being in charge.

2. He could start the termination process for employees who consistently fail to work according to standards. Yes, it's true that firing nonperformers involves time and trouble. But taking this important step sends a powerful message to subordinates: Around here everyone is expected to do an acceptable job. No one lies down on the job.

3. Paul could study the allocation of work. It is probably true that some employees have heavier work loads than others who read magazines and carry on long conversations with coworkers. Uneven distribution of the work is a frequent contributor to low morale and productivity.

4. He could consult with those colleagues who have been more successful in getting money for repairs and remodeling and try to find out what they did that he could emulate.

5. Paul could advise his boss in the home office that the uncoordinated calls and requests to the district office are creating havoc. Perhaps his boss could help Paul in working out a system with the home office that would be less counterproductive. Paul might even insist that the calls be funneled through him or his assistant.

6. He could offer to help his employees to set priorities for the work they have on their desks or the requests from the home office, instead of letting them guess about what is more important.

Paul isn't helpless, he just perceives himself to be. He has learned to be powerless.

When managers are powerless, there is, of course, a ripple effect. Almost everyone connected with them is made to feel helpless as well. The ripple effect can debilitate an organization. Everyone in an organization is susceptible to the ailment.

Some of the frequently observed characteristics of helpless people are

They externalize blame. There is a tendency to blame outside forces—higher management, other departments, the economy (frequent among salespeople), the system, etc. Since they are being done to, there must be someone out there doing it to them. They themselves are victims. They'll be quick to assure you that they don't deserve the treatment they are getting. "If only . . ." is a wistful statement heard frequently. "If only those other people would stop fouling me up."

They attribute the success of others to "politics." You may recall Paul saying that his more effective colleague "knows the right people." A familiar axiom is, "It's not what you know, it's who you know." Pity all of us talented, sincere, bright people. We are not valued. Basically it comes down to what connections one has. Influence is it.

They ensure their continuing helplessness. Paul will continue to send requisitions to the home office that no one honors. He will not take any other steps to supplement that formal requirement. Sometimes people in organizations stop doing even what the "book" calls for. What good will it do? they ask. In some extreme cases, people will subvert the system to keep it from functioning and thereby proving their powerlessness to be justified. A very frequent example: A manager has a bright, ambitious subordinate who comes up with an unusual way to get action. The manager squelches the bright subordinate, or transfers or terminates him or her.

TAKING CHARGE

Paul is typical of the many people in organizations who learn to be powerless and find ways to live with it, to the detriment of everyone who has to deal with them. Following are three case histories of people who, faced with difficult management challenges, took responsibility and exercised power to get what they wanted.

Case 1. Mel C. is a district manager for the same company that Paul F. represents. His office quarters are old as well. But there is a freshness about the office. Not only are the walls newly painted, but there is no dust, and there are no pieces of paper on the floor. Where Paul's subordinates appeared sullen, dispirited, and even inefficient, the employees in Mel's office reflect an optimism and a cheerfulness. At the time Mel took over, about six months ago, his office staff had many of the same complaints that Paul described. The problems have not all been solved, but Mel has taken steps to equalize the workload, has started termination proceedings on a few employees, has set up a system for all telephone requests from the home office.

After having been in Paul's operation, the visitor to Mel's office senses a very different atmosphere. People are friendly and helpful. They talk enthusiastically about their work. Clearly they reflect good feelings about the job, Mel, and themselves.

Mel is a very political person. He makes it a point

to know who does what in the home office, and he stays in touch with everyone. Although he is well aware that a natural competitiveness exists between home office and field, he doesn't let a them-versus-us tone enter his relationships. He clearly established himself as *the* district manager, and both his subordinates and home office people are expected to understand it. In the home office, Mel has the reputation of knowing how to get things done. There's one other thing that they say about Mel, that he never forgets a favor.

Case 2. Terry M. manages an internal consulting group for a large corporation that has been undergoing many changes since it was purchased by another large company a few years ago. The merger was not an easy one. There have been substantial changes in management and in policy. The old, comfortable ways that Terry and her coworkers knew under the old regime are gone. In a short time, the entire atmosphere of the company changed. The former management was somewhat paternalistic, easy going, careful to make sure that a creative spirit prevailed. What policies existed were sometimes bent for individuals, not always fairly. But there was a conviction among employees that they were valued and that their interests would be protected.

The new management seems less interested in the human side of management. In fact, they are viewed by many in the company as numbers-crunchers. Management has laid off a number of long-term employees, and has reorganized divisions, not always in ways that seem logical. There's much turmoil, and as can be expected, morale and motivation are low. Terry expresses the situation this way: "Some of my friends here say they come to work in the morning, do what they have to do, collect their pay, and go home. That's the extent of their involvement." Terry admits that she sometimes wakes up in the morning dreading to go to work.

But the difference between Terry and her co-workers is that she insists on maintaining performance standards. Motivation and productivity may suffer elsewhere in the company, but not in Terry's department. Her subordinates put in a full day, effectively. "We're taking on more assignments than we ever did. And we're completing them on time. I've never seen this group more productive."

Terry is a take-charge person. You have only to spend a few hours with her on the job to discern that fact. She could externalize. She could shrug her shoulders and, like some of her colleagues say, "What can you do? It's impossible to operate under these conditions." But instead Terry proves that it is quite possible. She is unusually sensitive to the needs of her employees. They are as uncertain, demoralized, and anxious as other employees in the company. She is available to them, keeps in contact, patiently listens to them when they need just to talk, and protects them as much as possible from the confusions and tension existing throughout the corporation. "I hold frequent meetings. I tell them as much as I can find out. I encourage them to bring rumors and gossip to me so that I can set them straight. And I make sure that what counts are my standards. That's their main concern—doing what I expect of them."

Case 3. Philip S. provides a power story that I have always found extraordinary because it demonstrates what a person can do to build influence and visibility when the deck seems stacked. Shortly after World War II, Philip went to work for a very large insurance company as a group insurance specialist. Although group insurance had been around since the 1920s, it was a relatively new product for Philip's company. He was one of the first in his division to open a sales office in the field. Three years after he established the office, he was called into the home office to replace the man who had hired him. When I met Philip, he was group sales manager, trying to build a national sales operation in a field in which most other large insurance carriers had already built a substantial base. Because of limited budgets, Philip decided to concentrate on per capita production rather than overall volume. That is, many of his field offices were staffed with only one or two people, whereas his competitors were building offices with as many as eight to ten group specialists, and in a few cases, even more. Philip's operation was not considered significant to the company's growth, and, in fact, Philip's division was located across town from the main office in an old factory. One definite plus on Philip's account was that he had a sponsor/mentor, an esteemed, experienced vice president.

But there were a number of minuses, enough to characterize Philip's base has having little power. The first was the aforementioned emphasis of the company that did not include group insurance. As a result, Philip's operation accounted for a relatively small portion of the company's volume, and not much of its profit. In fact, Philip's division ran in the red for some years, first, because of the cost of setting up a national organization, and second, because some basic underwriting proved to be costly. Philip's sponsor was kicked upstairs to a position of little influence. Another minus was the tradition of promoting actuaries for high positions. The fast track, for the most part, belonged to them, and the track lay through the reinsurance operation, which for many years had constituted the principal marketing thrust. Yet, despite the disadvantages of his position and credentials, Philip rose rapidly through the company to become chairman of the board.

There were several contributing factors to Philip's accumulation of power, even though at first he occupied a position that would leave many people feeling rather powerless. First, he had self-confidence; he was bright, and he knew it. He was not an intellectual, but he was shrewd. Second, even though he was somewhat isolated in a relatively unimportant division, he never acted accordingly. He established a very extensive network throughout the entire company, and the more people he knew, the better he felt about his ability to assume greater responsibility. Third, he always maintained the big view, he studied the corporation as a whole. Although he managed his own operation well, he made sure that he understood how the company worked, where the power centers were, who was a formidable competitor and who was not. Furthermore, he knew where he could expect to find support. For example, after he was promoted to vice president, he kept a list of everyone in the company who called to congratulate him. He assumed that those people who didn't were not interested in or willing to maintain an alliance with him.

OPEN VS. CLOSED SYSTEMS

Mel, Philip, and Terry certainly cannot be labeled passive people. Passivity is powerlessness. Not one of the three is a giant in any sense. They do share a desire to be in control of whatever they can. In interviews with them, it is obvious that they are uncomfortable simply reacting and adjusting to the conditions that exist around them. In addition to a "take charge" mentality, each of the three exhibited other characteristics.

Willingness to assume responsibility. Douglas McGregor, the psychologist who became famous for his Theory X-Theory Y, wrote in his book, *The Human Side of Enterprise,* that it was normal for people to seek responsibility. As I've stated, helplessness is for the most part learned behavior. A willingness to assume more responsibility, even though it may entail risk, is a sign of a desire to grow, to advance and make progress, which most people, according to Frederick Herzberg, a social psychologist known for his research in motivation, are motivated to do. The evidence is therefore growing in motivation research, in what makes people behave the way they do, that people like to take on greater responsibility because it is a sign that they are moving in a direction rather than standing still.

Sensitivity. They are very aware of what is going on around them. Terry demonstrates how sensitive she is to the needs of the people who report to her. Philip was tuned in to the relationships of people and operations in the company. Those relationships change, sometimes almost daily. It is hard work to keep up with them, but the pay-off is in being able to assess your relative position and to understand the dynamics that affect you and your job.

Organization view. Mel takes the view that everyone in the organization is or should be committed to the well-being of the whole. Many people by contrast are parochial and compartmentalized. They sit in their offices or at their desks, concerned only about what immediately affects them or is going on in the vicinity. Power-sensitive people know that you have to observe and analyze the organization as a whole if you really want to know what is happening to you today or might come your way tomorrow or the day after. More will be said later in the book on studying the power centers and the power track. For the moment, it is sufficient to point out that it is impossible for you to assess the power you have without seeing yourself in the overall context.

Networking. Philip made it almost a discipline to know everyone in the organization who might have influence or present a challenge. This is good practice. The more alliances you can form in the organization the better your chances of knowing what is going on and how you can benefit. Alliances add to your power. They constitute informal organizations that can when necessary spread information and apply pressure. Since you never know where all your help could come from, it's recommended that you know, and be known by, as many people in the organization as possible.

There's a general way to distinguish power-minded people from those who see themselves as powerless. The former are "open systems," reacting to their environments. They have boundaries, protecting themselves and their space or territory. But those boundaries do not block the entrance of information from the outside. It is essential for the open system to be alert to information from outside, because it is characteristic of such a system to adapt to external realities. All of this may seem abstract. It is less so when you reflect on your own organizational experience. If you have experienced a change of management, or just of a boss, you have received new information that points the way to how you can best work with this new manager or management. You receive the information (the input), process it, and make the appropriate adjustments, which is the output.

Closed systems have boundaries that are nearly impermeable, preventing them from interreacting with the environment. From the moment that the boundaries close, such systems start to deteriorate. They become obsolete, they continue to operate on old information that is becoming out of date. As a result, people whose systems are closed one day wake up and find that all opportunities have passed them by, that they may even be out of a job.

Or to put it another way, some people sit in their closed systems and say, "If only . . . ," and others, who are more open, wonder, "What if . . . ?"

3

PLUGGING INTO POWER SOURCES

You don't acquire power simply by saying, "Now I'll take charge!" However, there are a number of sources of power within your organization waiting for someone to plug into them. It can be you. Following is a description of the various sources of power that might be available. Not all of them will work in every organization. There are a number of factors—for example, the structure, culture, style of management, etc.—that help to determine which sources of power provide the most current.

POSITION POWER

Position is the most obvious source of power. But it is not absolute or automatic. Actually the power inherent in the box on the organization chart may be quite illusory and certainly vulnerable. Many a manager recruited from the outside by the promise of an impressive title and salary has found to his or her distress that there isn't much more. For example, you may move into a position previously held by a weak person who let the power drift away or passively watched others in the organization carve pieces out of it. Your boss may be extraordinarily powerful, and although you occupy a legitimate position, you find yourself very much in your manager's shadow. As you will see, that can give you some power if you take advantage of it, but it will have little to do with your title.

Time and changing values of the organization may affect the position power. Ten years ago, the job of manufacturing or production manager might have been quite significant in many organizations, but many corporations have gone into the service or knowledge industry. Manufacturing plays a smaller and smaller role. In one company I know, marketing was the power spot for years, since the president of this medium-size company had come up that path. When the president retired, the financial people took over, and the power and prestige of marketing were downgraded.

Some managers have been dismayed to find that, when they take over a position that should be powerful, not even their subordinates are prepared to give much respect. The subordinates have to be convinced that their new managers deserve their respect and loyalty. In many organizations, position power is contingent on the occupant's proving himself or herself and on subsequent strategies to expand the power base.

PERSONAL POWER

The power of a person, as distinct from that person's position in the organization, is hard to formulate. Some people create power by the force of their personalities. When I was a teenaged boy in a military school, I was envious of a certain kind of boy who, without showing superior intelligence or using intimidation, could mold a bunch of unruly adolescents into a disciplined group. From the outset of their appointment these young leaders displayed a confidence that people would follow them, that they had the power. I think self-confidence, such as these young boys displayed, is a factor that contributes to the building of power. If you believe that you really have it, that you deserve to have it, and that others will recognize that you have it, then you may indeed enjoy power.

Such self-confidence may be firmly based on your knowing who you are and where you are going, two important aspects of self-knowledge that will be discussed in a subsequent chapter. It may also stem from where you have been and what you have done. Your record of achievement may inspire your confidence in yourself and may invite the deference of others. If you have been successful, especially under fire, you are likely to continue to have faith in yourself. Of course, in your new circumstances, you must continue to display your skills.

Some people seem to project power by the way they appear, speak, or carry themselves. They come across as very strong. No doubt you have passed certain executives in the hall whom you didn't know well but who you noticed projected power. In the building where I worked for many years there was a large advertising agency on the lower floors. Frequently groups of people from this agency would get on the elevator, and certain of them would stand out. There was something that set them apart, and if they were on the elevator long enough, the deference of others toward them would become evident.

Years ago, a friend of mine, still in his thirties, abandoned a promising law practice to return to academia as associate professor in a large university, where I visited him. As we walked down the corridor of the building in which his office was located, we met some of his colleagues and stopped for brief conversations. Later I told him that I was struck by the unusual degree of respect that these other faculty members accorded him. He was skeptical, but I wasn't surprised to learn less than two years later of his appointment as dean of the law school.

Unquestionably physical appearance can aid in the projection of power. People of large physique (not fat!), who wear well-tailored and good quality clothes, who carry themselves erect and in a confident manner, do draw attention. Nevertheless, for them to hold the attention, and respect, of others, there needs to be substance behind the style.

AUTOCRATIC POWER

Autocratic power is also known as coercive. If you have been in the military, or can remember when you worked while going to school, you have probably encountered this kind of power. Most young people find bosses who like to take advantage of them. Entrepreneurial managers are very often autocratic. Recently a business magazine ran profiles of the ten "worst" bosses, and many of them were distinctly authoritarian, even screaming at and threatening employees.

Today's workforce generally has low tolerance of autocratic power wielding. As you will see later, there are times when pulling rank, being autocratic, is quite appropriate, even desirable. Otherwise, you have to have a support system for your coercive power. It helps if you provide exceptionally good opportunities for people to excel, pay extraordinarily high salaries, and have the only job opportunities within many miles. But if people have choices, if they can exercise freedom, they will usually reject this kind of power.

ASSIGNED/DELEGATED POWER

Assigned or delegated power comes from higher management. You may get it from your boss, or from your boss's boss, or from higher up. Many cases it is there, waiting for someone shrewd enough to tap it. Unfortunately many people make the mistake of waiting for it to be handed to them. Later chapters are devoted to showing you how to get power from above.

Of course, it is important to keep in mind that power that is given to you can also be taken away. Management itself can change and decide that your holding power doesn't fit in with the new plans, or management can simply change its mind about you and conclude that the power given you doesn't seem to suit you. Management can even decide someone else is worthier than you. In sum, you must never assume that what has been given you is yours to keep.

Yet, there are a number of ways to make delegated or assigned power yours. For example, you may exercise your power in a way that pleases higher management. Find ways to become indispensable by expanding your power base, forming alliances with other managers, increasing the loyalty, the commitment, the productivity of the people who work for and with you. Recommendations for doing these things will be found elsewhere in the book. In other words, get such returns on the investment of your new power that management will fear it cannot get the same results elsewhere.

Still, you may lose the power given you from above if you do not establish a firm base of power that is identified with you. You will undoubtedly wish to look at other power sources described in this chapter to help you do just that.

ASSOCIATIVE POWER

Just as you can have guilt by association, you can enjoy power the same way. If your boss is strong, just by being a key subordinate you can expect others to accord you a certain deference on which you can build your own power. (In fact, other people will hand you what you need to build your base.)

If you are seen as a protégé of a powerful executive, you can bask in the reflection. Another word to describe the relationship is sponsorship. You can benefit from having a sponsor who keeps you advised as to the opportunities for advancement, for expanding your authority, for putting your name before powerful people. Sometimes the relationship is all it takes for a person to acquire power. An extreme example of this was a young person brought into an organization with which I was familiar by the sales vice president who had been impressed by the young man at a convention both attended. The young man had a pleasant personality and was very bright, but he had little actual sales experience. Nevertheless he was put to work supervising the work of salespeople in the field, developing marketing strategies and sales aids, and training new salespeople. Some of his more experienced co-workers grumbled at the favoritism granted him and at the need for them to give him equal status. They were openly scornful of the quality of his work, which reflected his lack of experience. Eventually the embarrassed vice president had to terminate him when some of the veteran salespeople with whom he had worked in the field called to tell the executive that they would not work with him again.

In most cases, sponsorship relationships that are based on competence and promise work to the protégés' advantage. Of course, the associative power you enjoy in such a relationship will last only as long as your sponsor stays powerful and in the good graces of management. If for any reason the sponsor becomes discredited or considered "surplus," you might have some of that rub off on you as well.

A mentor relationship can also provide you with associative power. Knowing that an experienced, high level person with prestige and widespread respect favors you can add luster to your position and reputation. However, just as with a sponsor, you must be prepared to build your own base.

COMPETENCE POWER

When you know something that others need to know, you have power. When you have racked up an impressive record of achievement, you have power.

It is always good to find a niche for yourself in an organization, one that no one else occupies. Some years ago, a young man joined a large consulting firm to specialize in sales and sales management training for the firm's customers. After a time, he observed that the consulting group was weak in the area of management development specialists. He began to take advantage of every opportunity to acquire expertise in the subject, and when some big opportunities arose to apply what he had learned, he was ready. For a number of years, he was regarded by his associates as the firm's expert in both sales and management training. Eventually he left to form his own firm. His observation about his career with the large firm: "There's not a lot of security in that field. I watched people come and go for years, and I was able to hang on because I had what they wanted."

It is not enough to have valued expertise, you must also let people know you have it. You must have a PR program for yourself. In the case of the durable consultant, it was notable that he wrote many articles and spoke at a number of meetings of associations. He advertised himself in a way that advertised his firm.

In short, find some expertise that the organization needs *and values*, do it very well, and let everyone know you do it well. However, bear in mind that the values and needs of the organization change, and your areas of competence and expertise must reflect these changes.

Your performance also adds to your competence power. When you perform at an exceptional level for a sustained period, you accumulate a lot of points for yourself. As in the case of your special knowledge or skill, you have to keep calling attention to what you do. Organizations have short memories. It's not even "What have you done for us lately?" Rather, it comes down to, "What are you doing right now that we should care about?" Ironically, you can be so consistent about your superior level of work that people accept it—and lose sight of it.

For your own gratification and self-confidence, make competence your foundation for all other power. But do not rely too strongly on it alone.

RESOURCES POWER

When you have control of resources that other people in the organization need, you have power. A good illustration involves the early days of the computer. Look at the power the data processing manager had. He was in charge of the other priests in the temple, and from all over the organization, suppliants humbly approached. No one could quite understand what they did in the computer room. The language was mysterious. No one told the high priest what to do. They didn't understand the process that well. So they would say what they needed, or thought they needed, and ask for help. This gave the computer expert tremendous power. But since then, the computer has left the computer room, and much of that power has gone with it.

In a large eastern company, purchasing and supplies are centralized for purposes of efficiency. It makes sense to have one department storing and issuing supplies for everyone, instead of having twenty such operations spread throughout the system, doesn't it? Well, not if you're a department that has frequent shortages of much-needed supplies. Just look at the power that supplies department head has. If he or she doesn't care for you, if the department head feels aggrieved by you, your requisitions go unfilled. That is exactly what some department heads complain about.

In other companies, the legal department garners a great deal of clout. If the company enters into contracts on a frequent basis, the legal staff can hold things up indefinitely.

The message is that if you control resources—technical, financial, human, informational, material, etc.—that other people need, then you have power. If you want to increase your clout, look for resources that others need. They may be in unlikely places. I knew of one canny manager who had himself appointed new products manager. It was impossible to introduce a new product for consideration without going through him. And in that company, new products was the name of the game. Power!

ALLIANCE POWER

In order to gain alliance power it is important to look for coalitions to build. Several field managers for a large city agency in a midwestern metropolitan area had long complained that their central office treated them like orphans. The field managers discovered that, operating singly, they had no power. But when they all formed a managers' group and asked to speak and negotiate as a group, they suddenly found themselves being treated with unfamiliar respect. What they learned is that top management generally will not let go of any more power than they have to. But when they have to, they often will.

Look for people who share your interests. It is best not to include people from lower levels than yours. Management frowns on too much fraternization with the troops. Also, be careful to let management know that this is not a dissident or rump group. You are getting together in order to exchange knowledge and experience, to discuss common problems, and to trade solutions. You are an informal organization that is working to promote the aims of the organization.

However, from time to time you may want to schedule joint consultation sessions with higher management to give them information, or to solicit it. You do not have to resort to any strong-arm tactics in order to be acknowledged and respected by management. The fact that there is now a group of you rather than an aggregate is enough to make them take notice. They will probably tread warily rather than uncaringly.

Some managers have formed management clubs, ostensibly and actually to further their management skills. They hold meetings during business hours and occasional dinner meetings off premises. Certainly it is difficult for higher management to hinder professionals acting in a professional manner.

CHARISMATIC/VISIONARY POWER

It used to be said that one could not develop charisma, but that is probably not true. The visionary is charismatic. The visionary sees beyond the numbers and the people and equipment; he or she has a mission. And, I suspect, visionary abilities can be developed. It takes imagination, and all of us can feed our imaginative faculties. It is important because there is power there. People like visionaries, because most ordinary folk live lives of low expectations and sensitivity. Visionaries spark others, and provide excitement and meaning for them. They can be great fun to work for.

I knew some visionaries who were running a publishing company, except that in their presence you did not refer to it as such. They published newsletters and information for business executives. But again, in their presence, you did not call it information. They referred to their product as *intelligence*. It was their job, as they described it, to analyze the masses of data that could affect the well-being of business organizations and tell business people what they needed to know to run their companies. These visionary managers imbued their employees with a sense of profound importance: Thousands of executives out there depend on you to help them make profits. No, they did not run a publishing company. They were self-described intelligence analysts, "the CIA (when it was still considered a compliment) of American business."

What was especially interesting was that these visionary managers were not especially skillful as managers. They violated many of the "rules" for managing people. But they inspired tremendous loyalty and esprit de corps among their employees, who often used the word "exciting" in describing their work atmosphere.

As often happens in the evolutionary process, the visionaries were replaced by bureaucratic managers. The intelligence became information. The company became a publishing operation. The sense of mission disappeared, as did the excitement. The power shifted from the visionaries to the autocrats.

REWARD POWER

Anyone who is in a position to give a reward to someone else has power. Consider an extreme case, that of the president of a voluntary or professional association. The president of such an organization has very little position power. After all, you cannot order volunteers around or they will simply go home and not come back. As president, you are very much under the scrutiny of the board of directors or trustees. The record is public. But you have reward power. You have the power of appointment, for example. You have posts to fill, and some of those are prestigious and visible. The people you wish to reward occupy the choice spots.

If you are a manager with paid employees, you also have reward power. In fact, that is probably the only basis of your power. People will work well for you if they know they can depend on you for recognition of their performance. You distribute the merit increases, the responsibilities, the opportunities for visibility. You praise and confer prestige.

Furthermore, as you will see in a later chapter, if you use your reward power over subordinates wisely and fairly, you will find that your employees can add to your power with your management. They will help you to be a power within the organization.

You may have reward power even though you do not directly manage people. Assume that you are in a staff position such as training. You are responsible for training employees in a particular division in certain technical skills. The manager whose employees you are training is particularly helpful and supportive. She provides on-the-job continuing coaching after the formal training sessions. You write a letter praising her cooperation. That letter constitutes a reward for her, even though you are not on her level. Others such as marketing or financial people often have similar opportunities.

PROFESSIONAL POWER

You may be able to become prominent in a professional or trade association, and your visibility there will reflect well on you internally. However, make sure that your participation in the association is sanctioned by your organization. Some organizations encourage their people to get involved outside, regarding that participation as good public relations or as an opportunity for their people to expand their competence by their associations with professionals from other organizations. The more visible you become, the more publicity your organization can receive and that can hardly hurt you.

Somewhat allied with the professional association is the community or volunteer agency in opportunities to provide visibility. Getting involved with the United Fund or the symphony or Boys' Clubs can add to your prestige and that of your organization.

Writing articles or books and giving speeches or participating in workshops on your specialty is another way to build your professional power within your organization. The enlightened organization takes the view that as you become more widely recognized and applauded, so does it. Unfortunately many organizations are not so enlightened. You may well find, as you become more active outside, a lot of internal grumbling over your wasting your time and energy away from the job. Indeed, you will have to be especially sensitive to the possibility that others, particularly your own subordinates, will believe that you are neglecting your responsibilities.

The better known you become in your field and the more active you are outside the organization, the greater the possibility that you will arouse competition and sharpshooting inside the organization. You may increase your power. You may also increase your vulnerability.

There is compensation, however. When you become well known and highly regarded in your field, you will find someone else to welcome you if your own organization ceases to value you or if you lose out in a power struggle.

AVAILABILITY POWER

This kind of power is otherwise described as flowing from being in the right place at the right time. Another name for it is *opportunity* power. It is true that in some cases people happened to be in the right place when opportunity came along, but more often people prepared themselves for the possibility that they might someday be in the right place when opportunity came by. One such example is a young woman who for some years had been a technical skills trainer in a bank. She was interested in stocks personally, but she also detected that the banks were beginning to be interested in them as well, as they expanded their financial services. She took an intensive course to prepare for her stockbroker's license, took the all-day test and passed. Then she let it be known that she had acquired some new credentials. Eventually the bank for which she worked began to offer related services, and they needed someone who could train platform personnel in the branches how to market the new service. There she was. She had sensed an opportunity long before it was generally apparent, prepared herself for it, and was rewarded for being in the right place at the right time.

Availability or opportunity power is an excellent way to build your base, if only because many of your would-be competitors are lazy or shun risks. You hear people talk about how they would like to go into management someday, but how many of them actually begin to acquire management skills before the chance for promotion comes up?

Years ago I saw the advantage of being available. I worked at the time for Research Institute of America, a publisher of various kinds of newsletters. At the bottom of the totem pole, I was delegated the weekly responsibility to contribute a marketing piece to a general management newsletter. It was a terrible publication, poorly edited, lacking an identification and impact. Yet, I was fascinated. I wasn't sure how I would edit it, but I knew there was a lot of room for improvement and that somebody in management would see it. So I kept writing for it, even though some of my coworkers thought I was wasting my time. Eventually, the editor who was responsible for it was let go. The newsletter was up for grabs, and I grabbed for it. I was the only person who was both available to take on more responsibility and was a regular contributor. The move boosted my career enormously. But it was no accident. The next two chapters will be devoted to helping you to prepare to be available.

You can undoubtedly plug into other sources of power. The above are the ones you can expect to find in most kinds of organizations. They are also kinds of power that most people can use. Will or do most people? Probably not. If you are eager to, you will find yourself playing in a more elite league. You will have left most people behind. You will have taken important first steps to take charge of your life—and to have an impact on others.

But there are some important considerations to keep in mind. First, don't rely too much on one source of power. Take advantage of as many as you can. The greater number of sources of power you can tap, the stronger your power base will be.

Second, don't neglect competence power. That is the core of your base. If you are ever found lacking in the competence area, you can suffer a permanent setback in your progress. Granted, you will encounter some people who have tremendous skills in selling themselves—and that's all they seem to have to sell, but for them there usually comes a reckoning. The bill is much more than they can pay. Their careers are bankrupted.

Third, continue to test the reality around you. Managements change, missions change, organizations change, the environment changes. Your source of power may fail you or be shorted out. Bear in mind that to gain power, but especially to keep it, you must be extraordinarily sensitive and aware, characteristics that most of your potential competitors lack.

4

POWER CENTERS AND POWER TRACKS

Having identified the various sources of power, you need to know where you are most likely to find them in your organization. Looking at the table of organization of the organization chart is a first step. However, as has been pointed out, the titles and locations of the boxes may not tell you what you want to know. For example, George Arliss is senior vice president, and his box is just left and immediately below that of the president. The position looks powerful, but look more closely. Arliss is out of the line. He has a few staff functions reporting to him—personnel, training, and legal. Furthermore, he is 61 years old. You can reasonably conclude that Arliss has been kicked upstairs, especially if the post of senior vice president was created for him. Someone in power wanted to put Arliss in a relatively harmless position while the senior executive waited out his retirement.

All boxes on the same level are not necessarily equal. Paul Harrigan is one of six vice presidents. He has a title that doesn't indicate much: Planning and Development. Yet, the corporation has decided to experiment with venture groups that might develop into full-fledged entrepreneurial operations. If successful, the experiment could point the way to the future of the corporation. Paul is, as they say, sitting in the catbird seat. There is potentially a great deal of power there, although it is not indicated on the chart.

Thus, all positions on a level are not equal in power, and all lines do not give equal access to power. If you are considering the following sources of power, consider also whether they can be increased in potency in a certain power center or on a particular power track.

Position. The vice president of human resources probably does not have the prestige and clout that the vice president of marketing has. This extends to the people working for the vice president of human resources.

Assigned/delegated. If you are working in an organization in which most decisions are based on financial considerations, you can usually suspect justifiably that people in the financial line are considered more substantial than those in other functions. Whether or not they are objectively more important is not the issue. The value system of this kind of organization will place greater importance on what financial people in the organization do than anyone else.

Associative. If you are close to the person who is rumored to be the next president, you can bet that something is going to rub off.

Competence. If you are perceived as being very good at what you do, your importance will be much greater if what you are good at is what the organization most values. You may be one of the most effective training professionals in the world, but training people usually do not have much stature. If you are a specialist in mergers and acquisitions in an organization that is expanding, and you are good at it, then your competence will be more valuable to the organization than the training expertise.

Resources. Who gets to manage more, and has access to more? Two divisions may be of equal rank on the chart, but one has a larger budget, more people, more clout at the decision table, and more money to pay its people.

Availability. Clearly, being in the right place at the right time means more when your availability and the opportunity will lead to responsibility that is considered significant in the organization because it is connected with a power center or on a power track.

WHERE IS THE ACTION?

Here are some questions that can help you to identify those areas and routes upward that indicate where the power is concentrated. Your own strategies for accumulating power may be dependent on your present position relative to the centers.

What departments, divisions, or functions get the most attention? What group is the subject of frequent mention in the organizational newsletter or of laudatory, promising notices in the annual report? What group seems to receive a larger share of resources—money, people, space, equipment, etc?

What functions have been growing faster than others? This will give you a clue to where the organization is putting its dollars. Look for new facilities or for unusual mobility indicating frequent outgrowth of existing facilities.

Where have the promotions exceeded the normal or average rate? When new titles are created or proliferate, it's a sign of vitality and expansion.

In cutbacks, who suffers least? From time to time, almost every organization experiences some reductions, but favored or growth departments often receive less paring than others.

Where have the top executives traditionally come from? You may not be looking at the route to the top, but if you can pinpoint the track that many of them have followed, you will probably discover what functions or aspects of the operation are most favored, given the highest priority. Of course, priorities and values change. The last two presidents of a corporation may have come up through marketing, but now lawyers may be favored. For many years it was almost a given that insurance company presidents would be actuaries. That is not necessarily so anymore. In some high tech companies, presidents have been engineers in the beginning, but then succeeded by business types.

In short, study the past, the traditional path, but mix in your knowlege of what is going on now in the divisions that have not provided the top leadership; things may be changing.

What is the relative location of the divisions or departments? Growth departments or functions will usually (but not always) be in newer facilities more desirably located. Within the headquarters, they will often be more prominent in space, size, location, and so forth. They usually get preference when new or more desirable space opens up. In contrast, less valued aspects of the operation are less prominent, less conspicuous, less convenient.

Which part of the operation has the esprit de corps? People who sense that they are part of the power group reflect their feelings in their enthusiasm, competitive spirit, and, unfortunately sometimes, in their arrogance or abrasiveness. They talk like winners, act like winners. You may find a few of these individuals in any part of the organization, but in the power center, they are numerous.

Of course, the answers to the above questions have to be considered in the light of other information. What, for example, are the expressed strategies of the organization for the next three to five years? They may very well cancel out the conclusions that you have come to as a result of your own analysis.

Some organizations don't publish their strategic plans. Others don't even have them. So you must rely on the past and present. Always remember that when you project the past into the future, you are taking a chance. Perhaps, unknown to you, a small group of executives is meeting in secret session, planning to turn the company onto quite a different course, or perhaps next week another company will move in to buy out the present ownership.

Nevertheless, most companies, most organizations, operate in a fairly straight line. You can look at past practices, at traditional ways of doing things, and make certain assumptions about the future. But keep your antennae out.

WHO IS AT THE CENTER OF THE ACTION?

To further your search for power you need to study the people involved in the operations as well as the operations themselves. There are key individuals in your organization who enjoy greater power than others. If you are looking for the power track, to get close to a power center, for a sponsor/mentor, or for someone who could be an effective role model for you, these are the people you must locate.

Following are a number of indicators that might help you in your search. You may not want to rely too heavily on any one of them, but certainly if several apply to your candidate, you are most likely justified in saying, "There's one!"

Significant upward progress. The power center is not a shelfsitter. He or she has made rapid strides, probably moving significantly at least once every two years. However, don't assume that all of the progress must be vertical. Lateral moves also count in the game of mobility. Actually, mobility is the key word. If the person has moved, laterally or vertically, from one substantial responsibility to another, especially different kinds of responsibility, then you have a probable power center—and a power track indicator.

Consistently expanded responsibilities. Some people seem to be able to make omelettes from one egg.

They expand outward and upward. Give them a Luxembourg and they wind up with a France eventually. Look for these people. For the moment, at any rate, they are powerful. They have the resources and the influence to build empires.

Attendance at meetings. There are some people who are inveterate meeting goers, but the fact that they are invited by the powers is a tip-off. They may not have much line authority, but their power derives from their closeness to those who have. In one organization, a woman I know occupied no important position. She had a title that indicated nothing. She had no subordinates. Yet, she was a protégé of the president, who invited her to attend almost every significant meeting. She had the ear of the president. She knew almost everything that was going on. People who were aware of her power cultivated her, with justification.

Sign memos. Who originated many of the memos about policy, personnel changes, and the like? Don't disregard such signers simply because they might be in unlikely power spots. Years ago many employees at a medium-sized company began to see company-wide memos issued by the personnel manager. Usually personnel managers don't have much clout, but it soon became apparent that this one did. He had been hired by the chairman of the board because he seemed to reflect the chairman's values. In time he became the spokesman for top management. People who ignored or discounted him later found themselves shunted into less important positions or terminated.

Has up-to-date information. If a person's information is inclusive, even exclusive, certainly up-to-date, it's safe to conclude that person has access to a source of power.

Impressive office decor. There have been a lot of jokes made about qualifying for the water carafe, the extra window, or the Persian on the floor. But, as with many perennial jokes, there's truth to this. Corner offices with fashionable and tasteful trappings bespeak power.

The company of the top brass. There are people who are frequently seen conferring with or being consulted by high level management. Chances are they share some of the power, which is why they stay close.

Reporting relationships. Who reports to whom? Look at the context in which some people operate. They have talented, strong people as subordinates. In some cases, of course, it is not true, but company gossip will reveal this. If gossip does not discount such a manager, then chances are good that he or she is strong. If that manager reports to someone else of prominence, then you have a power cluster. I can't emphasize too strongly the importance of listening to gossip for this reason. I once knew a manager who was sandwiched between strong supervisors and professionals, and one of the founders of the company, who was a genuine visionary and one tough customer. Nevertheless gossip was very clear: this manager was the slab of baloney. In most organizations, over a period of time, gossip will rather accurately portray the personnel.

Frequent notice. Listen for the names that get mentioned regularly. You can depend on there being good reason for such notice.

Quoted frequently. Even better than having your name mentioned frequently in company gossip is being quoted. People won't quote someone for very long unless they have established importance and credibility. So if you begin to hear a certain name pouring out of the rumor mill, take note. You may be witnessing the evolution of a new power center.

Sought after. Picture a company or office party. Enter a well-known manager. Almost immediately he is approached by one or more people. In fact, he is probably never alone. And if he is much sought after by his peers, you have a definite sign that they regard him as important and powerful.

Sometimes people on a peer level will seek the cooperation, even the endorsement, of one of their own. This is their tacit admission that he or she is perceived as more powerful and influential.

Introduced with fanfare. Sometimes power centers are brought in virtually intact from outside. Watch for the new person who is introduced with much fuss and who, during the orientation period, seems to retain the respect of people around him or her. Often someone who comes in with a big flash just fizzles or is subsequently ignored, but a new person who shows staying power is worth noting.

New projects. A few people will have their pick of the new projects and enviable responsibilities. There will be patterns: When there is a prestigious job opening up, Old George will usually be asked to take it on, or there may be two or three who are frequently in the running. Label them power centers.

Comfortable with power. They talk knowledgeably about what is going on, they carry themselves confidently, they never appear harried and haggard. They wear the mantle of responsibility quite comfortably. Again, listen to gossip. Is there substance as well as style?

Shelfsitting. People who are taking up space and waiting out time become obvious. They may occupy positions that should be powerful, but you will find out through the grapevine—or from watching their comparative inactivity— that they no longer have any clout. They probably don't care.

In the case of shelfsitting, look for the real power. In some instances, there may be a vacuum. If so, watch to see who moves to fill it. Where there is power, what are the relationships that sustain it? Chances are the shelfsitting boss is being bypassed. Which subordinate is really running the operation? He or she most likely is someone to keep an eye on—and respect.

Power watching is a matter of knowing who has a record of accomplishment—and continues to build it; who seems to know everything that is going on and is in on many of the important decisions; who consorts comfortably with the powerful. In short, it means keeping your eyes and ears open to see who in the organization can be useful to you in building your own base of power.

5

GETTING ON
THE POWER TRACK

A primary reason for wanting to build your power, for committing yourself to the power track, is to gain control over as much of your working life as you can. You don't want to spend the rest of your career dependent on someone else's wishes, reacting to and defending your rights against other people's bids for power, passively accepting the working conditions that other people impose on you, and accommodating yourself to the limitations set by others.

An important step in the acquisition of power is to know where you want to go. Do you have goals? The mere question evokes groans. I have long contended that if I were to stop ten people on the street randomly and ask them whether they had set goals for themselves for the next three to five years, nine would reply that they hadn't. They would probably say that they should have goals, but that they just hadn't gotten around to setting them. I'm not talking about lifetime goals. That's a bit much to expect in these fast-changing times. But you really ought to know where you'd like to be headed in the next few years. And if you do know that, you're already ahead of most other people.

Unless you have goals, you can't really say that you're in control of your life. Goals fulfill a number of needs:

They give order and structure. Abraham Maslow in his famous hierarchy of needs defined these as safety needs, just above food, drink, sleep, and sex. We all require some order and structure in our lives.

They provide a target. Achievement of your goals is something to work for. The very existence of them, sitting out there, can impart excitement. To be able to say, "In three years, I shall be . . ." or "I shall have . . ." is a strong motivating force.

They measure progress. Most of us need to have a direction. We don't enjoy merely marking time. When we recognize and work toward goals, we get a sense of movement. We can see where we are going and the pace.

They give a sense of achievement. Frederick Herzberg (of the two-factor theory referred to earlier) identifies achievement as a motivator. People take pride in their accomplishment.

They provide closure. Most people like limits, projects that come to an end. Too many open-ended activities can be frustrating and leave the feeling that one is not really getting anywhere.

GETTING TO KNOW YOURSELF

In order to work for you, your goals must be *realistic*. They must reflect your strengths, talents, and skills. If you set goals that reflect an ideal you, you will only become frustrated.

Your goals must also be relevant to the organization in which you will be fulfilling them. You have to look at its needs, desires, and direction.

Finally, your goals must express what you want for yourself, what is important to you. This is another reason why you must learn to know yourself thoroughly.

Goals are not the only justification for taking inventory of yourself. Since much power is negotiated, if you are to achieve lasting power, it means that others must be willing to let you have it. When you draw power from them, they give it up. They must see a reason for giving it up. Thus, you are, in effect, selling yourself as worth ceding power to, and they are buying you.

No salesperson can be successful selling what he or she does not understand. This sales principle applies to you as well. You are a product that you need to know inside and out. This is an on-going study because you change and the "market" changes. Most people fail to conduct on-going studies of themselves. They lose touch, and then lose power.

In trying to develop a personal profile, people frequently resort to measuring themselves against others, especially those in similar jobs: how well they get along with bosses, how popular they are, whether they get the really good opportunities, and what others think of them. However, comparisons of this kind are not at all reliable in determining your true identity. Instead, they can cause you to lose sight of the real you for the following reasons.

Minimization. You may tend to focus on unimportant differences between you and your colleagues—how you dress, for instance, or who goes to lunch with whom, may become a matter of prime importance. The truly important factors, such as education, experience, skills, work attitudes, ambitions, and perceptions are often lost in the shuffle.

Exaggeration. You may feel that your coworkers are doing better in their jobs than you are in yours, and this may cause you to exaggerate your deficiencies (or what you believe are your deficiencies). Conversely, you may unduly inflate your own performance. In either case, you've missed the truth.

Imitation. If you see a coworker doing something very well, you may decide to try to imitate him or her. For example, a coworker may do a great deal more talking than you do at staff meetings. You believe that she is more successful than you because of this visibility she receives. You try to copy the style, even though your verbal strength has always been the crisp opinion delivered at the right moment. Obviously, such behavior takes you away from the real you.

Oversensitivity. You may pay too much attention to what others tell you about yourself. Since these opinions are inevitably based on some degree of personal bias, you are receiving a distorted picture. Thus, criticism, explicit or implied, can lead you to assume that you have a major defect in your character. On the other hand, praise from someone else can have you believe you are a genius. In either case, judgments about yourself based on this feedback will be inaccurate.

Assessing yourself accurately isn't easy. It's normal

for you to have blurred vision. To help you get a better profile of yourself, follow these steps.

1. *Look at your failures.* I heard Peter Drucker, the famed teacher, author, and consultant, say once that you can't know what you can do until you know what you can't do. Thus your failures are important to you in assessing yourself. I'm talking about clear-cut failures where there is objective evidence that labels what you did (or did not do) as a failure. You may have come out of the experience suspecting that the skills required to be successful in the task or assignment were beyond your interests and abilities.

2. *Look at your triumphs.* Consider those jobs, tasks, and assignments that you have done outstandingly well, the accomplishments that have earned you merited praise. You enjoyed the experience, and even though you might have felt you needed more training, education, or practice, you were a natural.

3. *Measure your assets.* Looking at your failures and triumphs gives you a profile of your highs and lows. Now examine those functions that you practice frequently, perhaps so much so that you take them for granted. Ask yourself the following questions:

- Which of your principal job functions and re- sponsibilities do you perform the best?
- What do others, especially your boss, fre- quently call on you to do?
- What functions or tasks do you do that others in your department no longer try to do be- cause you are so good at them?

The point is what you do best is usually what you like most, and the work that others call on you to do—or at which they acknowledge your skills by not competing with you—is further evidence of your particular strengths.

- What functions did you perform or skills did you acquire in previous positions that might be useful to you in your career progress?
- Which of your functions do you feel unsuited to perform?
- Under what conditions do you feel you work best?
- How would you describe your working relationships with peers?
- Would you say that you have an optimum commitment to your work?

On the one hand, you would not describe yourself as a workaholic, and on the other hand, you do a good job of controlling conflicts between your work and personal lives.

- How good are your communicating skills— speaking and writing?
- What functions could you perform better if you had more training?
- What kinds of skills or talents do you have that are either unique in your department or superior to those of coworkers?
- How would you describe your major weaknesses?

Now that you've developed a list of areas in which you feel you have some qualifications and areas in which you are less skilled, perhaps the first thing you should do is be starkly realistic about the weaknesses. Ask yourself whether they are important to your career. If they are, make a note to do something about them.

There will probably be some weaknesses that you've always intended to do something about. The same applies to your strengths. There may be some that you've never really developed into practical skills. Obviously this does not mean that you should embark on a program to eliminate every weakness and develop every skill. The time and money required to turn aptitudes into skills must be considered. If you establish priorities, based on what really interests you and on profitable applications for new strengths, you will find it easier to take the first steps toward self-development that will help you gain new responsibility and influence.

In planning your progress for the next few years, to become a more powerful person, you need to start with your own needs, which generally will correspond to your potential and what you know you enjoy doing. Look again at the profile of your strengths and weaknesses. What kinds of work do you enjoy doing most? What gives you the greatest feeling of accomplishment? What are your goals? Power, yes. But money, too? To achieve expertise in a specialty? To acquire responsibility for the work of others? To earn the esteem of your colleagues? To gain professional prestige? Here are some considerations to help you clarify your objectives:

> 1. Assume that you have to quit your job. Ask yourself what the one thing is about the job that you most hate to give up. Write it down. Now make note of the thing you regret leaving behind second most, and so on.

2. List the five most important things you do in your job. First rank them in order of importance, then in the order of your enjoyment of them. You might also want to compare these entries with those on your "most hate to give up" list.

3. List the aspects of your job that you talk most about. Put down the things you say when someone asks you to describe your job.

These lists should alert you to what gratifies you, to what you should spend more of your time doing, and to what potential you have that can be actualized.

You have managed, by doing the above exercises and asking yourself the above questions, to accumulate a fair amount of data about yourself. How can you bring it all together? Here's the unifying step.

Describe in detail what your work would be like if you had the ideal job. How would you spend your time? What would your functions and responsibilities be? Apply the 3R test:

1. *Realistic.* In terms of your experience, your strengths and weaknesses, your likes and dislikes, is your ideal job description realistic? Is it possible for you to aim at such objectives?

2. *Relate to you.* Are your objectives functions and activities that are truly important to you, or are they what you think you should aim for? "Shoulds" are suspect, they may be left over from what others have advised you

through the years. Think in terms of what is meaningful *for you*.

Now that you have begun to classify the data in terms of what *you* can do well, want to do very much, and what you could do with more training, you must take a hard look at the last R:

3. *Relevant.* Are your objectives consistent with those of the department or overall organization? Use the following points to assess the relevancy of your goals:

Organizational changes. From your present point of view, what departments or divisions might be phased out or merged? What new managerial or professional positions are contemplated?

Staffing changes. What internal expansions or cutbacks might be undertaken in the next two or three years? Where will they be most likely to occur? How will they affect you, positively or negatively?

Technological changes. Consider your industry in particular, and technology in general. What could happen technologically to create new jobs, skills, organizational structures, etc.?

Budget changes. Where do you think the money will be spent in the next one to three years? Where do you think funds may be restricted?

New facilities. The construction of a new plant, laboratory, or research center might offer significant opportunities for advancement.

New projects or plans. The launching of a new product line, for example, could open doors.

The above are just some of the significant developments that could spell opportunity. Your concern, in your quest for more power and more control, is to make yourself ready for any of the above contingencies. People who avail themselves of opportunity power—being in the right place at the right time—have sometimes prepared themselves for months or years to be able to do so.

Your planning and goal-setting will help you to:
- Know what you have to offer.
- Know where you are going.
- Know what it takes to get there.

Of such is power made.

6

PERSONAL POWER: BECOMING INFLUENTIAL

There is a finite amount of power in an organization. It is not there for the taking; it is however there for the giving. People will cede power to you if they believe that it is in their interest to do so. You must sell them on the idea that it *is* in their interest. You are a salesperson. You have a product to sell, yourself, a plan, your talents. That is why it is so important for you to know yourself, to know what you are selling.

See yourself as selling much of the time. Most people do not admit that they engage in selling. Occasionally, of course, when they want a raise, a favor, or approval from higher management, they grant the need to be cast in a selling role. But if you are pursuing power, you are selling almost all the time.

Begin to see your contacts with others as potential transactions, much as the professional salesperson does. Even the most casual conversation is a transaction. You want something as a result of it. For example, you meet the president in the corridor and stop to exchange pleasantries. Immediately you have an agenda. If the president doesn't know you very well, you want to make a good impression so as to become more memorable. If the president is well acquainted with you, you want to further his impression that you are not only a very fine person but an exceptionally competent and confident member of the team. Before an important interdepartmental meeting at which you expect to play an important part, you drop in on two or three of your colleagues. You want to sound them out without being conspicuously partisan. You also hope to establish a good rapport that will carry over into the meeting, where, out of good will, they will give you support. You walk around your department and talk with your employees about themselves, their families, their concerns. You want to create the atmosphere in which they will feel free to alert you to hidden problems. You also want to leave the impression that you are a caring manager.

You use selling skills to build influence among your peers, and to gain the favor of higher management. Selling techniques enable you to advance yourself and your ideas, to disarm your opposition, and to resolve or reduce conflict. In a group decision-making situation, they can be invaluable to you in persuading the group to give you the results you want.

These skills have special significance for the manager of today's workforce, which increasingly responds to *sell* rather than tell. Employees want to be considered seriously, to be persuaded and negotiated with. Managers who deal with their employees in this mode usually get greater productivity and loyalty from employees. You can also get power from your subordinates. When they produce for you, they help make you a force to be reckoned with in the organization, and your subordinates can become significant advocates for you.

CHARACTERISTICS OF THE INFLUENTIAL

Some people are better at building their influence than others. I have identified some of the characteristics of the better persuaders:

1. *They know what they want.* They have goals, and they don't lose sight of them. They want to win, but they are realistic enough to know that they cannot consistently win at the expense of others.

2. *They know they have a right to try to get what they want.* You don't necessarily have the right to get your plan approved, your solution accepted, your ideas adopted, or your promotion granted, but you certainly have the right to speak your mind, to offer yourself or your ideas, and to try and sway the opinions and judgments of others.

3. *They are articulate.* Not only do the influential know what they want, they know how to express those wants and needs in terms that others can accept. They are careful not to create barriers to understanding.

4. *They are sensitive.* Successfully influential people are sensitive to what others might want from and contribute to the transaction. They are skillful at sensing verbal and nonverbal meanings. They strive to involve others who have something to contribute to the transaction—knowledge, experience, ideas, needs, and

resources. All this can be helpful in getting a desired result. If no effort is made to involve the other person, there will be little or no communication and understanding; certainly there will be no influencing.

Experienced influential people are sensitive to time and situation. There is a time and place for everything, and they are ever alert to how, when, and where to pursue certain actions, decisions, or requests.

5. *They have credibility.* Influential people develop a reputation for dealing squarely. Without abandoning their own interests, they are careful not to ride roughshod over others'. When you pursue power, you cannot expect to win friends, but you must be respected and trusted. Real believability takes time to build, but not long to destroy. You may make mistakes in judgment, and people will probably forgive you for them. But if you are proven guilty of deception or falsification, you may find your credibility shattered beyond repair—and your quest for power.

Credibility is much more important than likeability. In fact, some powerful influential people I've known are not warm and genial. They may even be gruff and distant. But in working with them, you are confident that they will not ignore your interests in their transactions with you. This is how they persuade you to give up some of your power to them.

6. *They know how to deal with opposition.* Although most people do not, the successfully influential anticipate opposition and know how to handle it. They may even welcome it, because overt opposition is easier to deal with than opposition that remains hidden. Also

opposition openly expressed can be tested and verified. If it is well-founded, the influential person can learn from the opposition and know what he or she has to do to overcome it.

7. *They know how to ask for action.* A satisfying transaction has a beginning, a middle, and an end. Transactions that don't close can be very frustrating to the people involved. Those good at using influence let others know what they want. If they want a piece of a new project, collaboration on an interdepartmental problem or task force, or to take on greater responsibility, they ask "for the order."

Chances are you've spent time with a co-worker talking about this or that, or sat in a meeting in which another participant went on and on, and you have wondered what on earth the person wanted. What was the bottom line? At the right time, a good persuader will let you know. He or she knows that you want closure too.

8. *They know what motivates others.* When people decide to take a course of action, there have been two factors that have influenced them: (1) the value to them of choosing that course of action, and (2) the probability that in choosing that particular course of action, they will get the result or the reward they seek. Confronted by two or more options, people tend to select the one that is more valuable to them—and more attainable. When you are trying to persuade other people to collaborate with you on a project, it is not enough to tell them that is a good thing to do, you must show why it is good for them. The successfully influential uncover

value and make it possible for others to have and enjoy it.

In summary, when persuaders have an idea, proposal, or opinion that they want others to buy, they

- make it interesting so people will listen;
- make it valuable so it appeals to the self-interests of others;
- make it easy so it seems feasible.

THE RULES OF PERSUASION

There are certain rules you must follow if you wish to influence and exert power over others (as well as draw power from them).

1. *Know your product.* What idea, project, solution, or opinion are you selling? Whatever you are selling, know what you have to offer. What are the strengths, the benefits? Why should others buy you or your ideas? You cannot reasonably hope to influence anyone on anything unless you can first convince them that you know what you are talking about.

An important part of knowing your product is being able to anticipate how those whom you hope to influence view it. For example, if you are aiming for a more responsible position in the organization, you are the product. You know what the responsibility entails, and you are confident you can handle it, but how do the decision makers see you? They have to let go of power before you can take it. How do they judge your strengths, your abilities, your performance?

2. *Know your prospect.* You have to know some-

thing of the other person's needs and wants if you are to negotiate successfully. You have to translate what you want into benefits that are attractive to the other person. What part of your proposition will most interest him or her? How would you describe those benefits? What kinds of words would you use? Is this a good time for your prospect to hear what you have to say? Would the prospect be more receptive at another time in another place? What tone of voice should you use? How detailed should you be? Should your approach be formal or informal, friendly or professional? The answers to these questions, and ultimately your effectiveness, are to be found in your knowledge of the other person. Remember, the other person is not about to give you what you want unless it is in his or her interest to do so.

Also keep in mind that the influencing will not take place entirely on a rational level. Your listener will respond to you in a number of ways—rationally, emotionally, psychologically, and intuitively. It is essential to anticipate these responses. People have biases, psychological predispositions, and preconceptions to which you must be sensitive. They can work for or against you.

3. *Involve your prospect.* Communication should not flow one way. The other person brings biases, strengths, needs, and desires to the interaction. You must listen for them, for they may affect your getting what you want. You also need to get feedback on whether you are influencing them. So take the prospect's temperature from time to time. Ask questions designed to get the prospect to tell you his or her reaction to what you are saying: "What's your reaction so far?" "Does what

I'm saying make sense to you?" "Do you agree with me that this might be a possible solution to the problems we've been having?"

Another reason you need to keep the other person involved is that otherwise they might stop listening to you. Most people are not trained to listen, and they need your help. So get them involved, and keep them tuned in. Your questions will tell you what they've heard.

4. *Ask for action.* Don't hestiate to ask the other person what you want from them as a result of the transaction, whether it be help, a recommendation, collaboration, advice, or acceptance of your ideas. Spell it out. A confused prospect does not buy; don't assume that your prospect knows what you want.

Asking for action, as I've pointed out, provides closure for both of you. Closure is both natural and desired. Experienced salespeople will tell you that they work for a "no." That means they will push the transaction as far as they possibly can in order to get closure, even if it means being turned down.

5. *Be prepared to handle opposition.* When two people meet to discuss something that is important, there will probably be some initial disagreement. It can arise because the prospect doesn't understand you clearly. Also, opposition to new or foreign ideas is to be expected. Few people listen attentively, surmount their biases easily, and surrender to someone else's ideas. A positive way to look at opposition is to recognize that the person fighting you is involved.

Building your ability to influence others involves knowing certain techniques and applying them consistently. You have to be aware of them, with the intention of using them, and use them skillfully.

TUNING IN TO THE HERE AND NOW

Effectively influencing others consists of more than practicing certain persuasive techniques. Although these techniques are very important, a base is necessary on which these techniques can be built. That base is awareness. Maintaining an awareness of what you want from, and what is happening in, a transaction is fundamental to successful persuasion.

If you do not maintain this awareness, you lose control. For example, you hear about an important new project to be undertaken by the company. You'd like to be involved with it, even head it up. You schedule an appointment with your boss to tell him you would like to be considered. It isn't your boss's decision. He'll have to discuss your bid with the executive vice president. "Right now, he's out of town," he tells you. "I know because I checked this morning to see whether I could see him on another matter. I think he's due back on Thursday. That's the day I have a budget session. Do you know how many meetings I have to sit through just to get a budget made up? I hate this time of year. Why, I'll bet you that I spend close to 40 percent of my time in those blasted budget sessions. Maybe I could see him on Friday, but that's iffy. I think the president wants to talk to me about something. He asked me to set aside the time. Then next week I go away . . ."

The boss, for one reason or another, does not seem to want to advance your bid. You don't know for sure because you didn't really find out whether your joining the project met any of his own needs, you didn't involve him. You did however ask for action, and you are getting opposition now, even though you may not recognize it as such. You aren't persuasive because you lack awareness.

You go to a colleague with whom you have strained relations. You want to mend fences in order to work together more effectively. After a few minutes of talk, she mentions that a week ago she made a proposal that would have solved the problem, and that you ignored it. You feel stung; you don't remember that she advanced a serious solution, and you certainly didn't mean to ignore it. For the next five minutes, you argue about whose perception is correct. At the end of the debate, you are both so out of sorts that you agree to talk at some later date when you both feel more positive. You failed to do what you intended because you lost your awareness of what was going on in the transaction.

One of your employees has been coming to work late rather consistently. You ask her into your office for a talk about her tardiness. She tells you that she has had problems keeping her four-year-old in nursery school because the child's father, from whom she is separated, is unreliable about paying the tuition. She has talked to her lawyer about it, but there's been no resolution. You wind up the interview expressing your hope that she gets her problems sorted out soon so that she can come to work on time.

Again, you lost your awareness and your control. You allowed yourself to get sidetracked in each of these three instances. You didn't get what you wanted, and you didn't gain power.

Answering the following questions can help you develop and maintain your awareness of the purpose of the transaction.

1. *What do I want from this transaction?* Do you want information, help, an agreement, some form of action or commitment? You will have a specific objective in mind, in most cases, but you look for other results as well. You want to know that you are communicating clearly, that you seem honest and sincere. You would like the other person to see you as pleasant and interesting to work with. You want to be admired and respected. You would like this transaction to add a block to your power base, and it will if it begins or continues a relationship that is seen as mutually beneficial.

2. *What do I think the other person would like?* Remember that power is negotiated and is ceded only when there is good reason to do so. Obviously your listener wants to spend time wisely and at least learn something from the conversation. He or she probably has a specific objective, too, although that objective may not have been there at the beginning. Much depends on how well you express your agenda and the benefits of going along with you. The other person would like to get a good deal if possible, and that means you have to provide the facts and the motivation to do business with you. He or she would like to feel that it is possible to rely on and trust you. Finally, the other person would like to believe his or her prestige, standing, self-worth,

and other needs to be enhanced by what goes on between you.

3. *What is going on at this moment?* It is important not to be so preoccupied with what you are saying and doing that you lose sight of the clues that the other person is giving. Is your listener interested, absorbed, or even thinking about what you are saying? Are you being as effective as you can be? Are you trying to relate to the listener, to involve the other person? How can you get a reaction or more participation? Does the other have knowledge, opinions, or experience that you should try to tap at this time? If you don't have some idea of what is going on at all times with the other person and with yourself, then you are not in control of the situation, and you both could be going nowhere.

4. *How does what is going on between us help us both to get what we want?* If you want it to lead to some kind of action, you must sense the effectiveness of what is happening now. How does it contribute to obtaining the objectives you both want? If you don't know that, the conversation may go off course and never get back on course. To be truly in control of the situation, to be able to guide the transaction to its desired conclusion, you must be constantly aware that what happens at any given moment either contributes to that desired course of action or leads away from it.

Since your objective is to influence others—their thinking, their decisions, their actions—you must learn to ask these questions automatically. If you don't have a clear objective in mind, and stick with it, you may have to settle for what you can get (and that may be what the other person wants from you). Think back to the three examples of transactions that preceded this section. In this first example, you wound up buying your boss's product: he wanted out of advocating your case. With your colleague, you engaged in a skirmish that took precedence over winning the war. And you totally lost out with your subordinate; you wanted her at work on time, but you ended up giving her carte blanche to continue being late.

I repeat that controlling is not dominating. It is important to control; it is undesirable to dominate. When a person dominates a transaction, he or she is usually the only one to achieve genuine closure, a satisfaction often gained at the expense of others. The dominator's agenda and objectives are most important. Thus a dominator may force a decision, interrupt others, argue, manipulate, push everyone else either by position, authority, or overwhelming personality, along a predetermined path. The key definition of controlling is guiding. When you control you know where the conversation should go. If it veers, you get it back on track. You can only do that if you remain aware of your objective, the other person's agenda, and where the transaction is at any given time.

GETTING A COMMITMENT

Very often what you want from another person in a transaction is some kind of commitment, preferably one that doesn't put you in debt. When you build power, you can create a lot of IOUs. The fewer you incur, the better. Take the following situation:

You are the executive in charge of data processing.

Another company executive has informed you that he has a special order that he needs in a short time. He asks that you clear your schedule and give his order priority. You both agree that he will send his batch to you first thing in the morning.

But the following morning the work doesn't arrive. When you call him, he apologizes for the delay and assures you the batch will be there momentarily. But you wait in vain. Again you call, and again he tells you the work is on the way. But it does not arrive.

This time, you tell him: "You asked me to clear my schedule, and I did. But I have five highly paid specialists sitting around. I'm upset. Because of your delay we have been idle for more than an hour. This is costing us a great deal of money, and it makes me look bad. Would you please get the work here now, in the next fifteen minutes?"

That's a straightforward statement. The only problem is that it is relatively powerless. The statement is couched as a favor. Suppose that, instead, after talking about how much it costs, and how bad you look, you said, "If your order is not here in the next fifteen minutes, I'll have to start another order. Yours will have to wait for the next break in the schedule."

That's a power statement. You described what was going on, the delay; you described your feelings about it, you're upset; you told the other manager what kind of change you want, an end to the delay; and you spelled out the benefits of that change to him, he gets his work done on time. Otherwise, he waits.

That's a typical, assertive—and probably effective—statement. It works because you confront an issue, not a personality. The issue is clearly drawn, that the batch was not delivered as promised. You might have suggested that the manager was not trustworthy, but that would have drawn you away from the issue and mired you in a debate about personality. Powerful people find it safer to deal with issues and facts, not soft areas such as personality.

Being assertive helps you to take control of an interaction. You can then guide it to your desired conclusion, in this case, an immediate change of behavior in the other person. When you are assertive and make your objective known, you have a better chance of getting what you want. You may not always get exactly what you want, but by stating your objective, you let the other person know where you stand. There is room for negotiation.

Consistent assertive behavior brings you more than the immediate results you want. When you are usually assertive, you acquire a reputation as a person who is straightforward, a person who says, "This is what I see. This is how I feel about it. This is what I want." People come to believe that they know where they stand with you. You are not seen as a manipulator or dominator.

Assertiveness increases your influence with others. They know that in a transaction with you they can get right to negotiating. They don't have to expend valuable time and energy wondering whether you are completely honest with them.

When people realize that what they see is the real you, they tend to listen more intently, to grant you more of their attention. Once people listen carefully to what you have to say, you are well on the way to exerting a greater influence over them.

Finally, your assertiveness encourages people to want to work with you. They don't have to wonder what your position is on an issue. They don't have to worry about your attacking them personally, since you have acquired a reputation for sticking with the issues. They don't have to try to interpret your real feelings, since you reveal them yourself.

All in all, you are a person others can believe in and trust. Being assertive doesn't necessarily win you friends. After all, you probably tell people what they would rather not hear. They don't have to like you, but they certainly will respect you and want to work with you. You will be on your way to getting more of the results you want more often. You will be building your reputation as a power person.

However, assertiveness may not always get you commitments of others. For example, go back to the executive who did not send the work to you. On a second occasion, he repeats his plea that you give priority to his work, and again he is late in getting it to you. You can be assertive again, but you don't have the commitment for the future that you would like. After all, you can't take his word that he will be on time the next go-around. So you say to him, "This is the second time you've asked me to clear my schedule, and then caused me inconvenience by being late. It upsets me very much. I feel it is an imposition on my department. When I called you about the delays, you always seem a bit embarrassed about the situation, so I would guess that you're not blasé about it. Let me put it to you this way. We have a problem. You would like your work done quickly when you need it, and I would like to be able to do it for you. I'm not happy about the way you reserve time and then fail to meet it. And if you're not happy, then we ought to agree that we both have a problem. What can we do about it in the future?"

Once again, you described the situation and how you feel about it, but you're also seeking information. Does the other manager feel unhappy also? You're involving the other person in the effort to find a solution. You recognize the other has resources to bring to the hunt for a solution. The change of behavior, in you, in him, in both of you perhaps, that contributes to the solution will benefit both of you.

You are being *responsive* as well as assertive. Where assertive behavior gives information, responsiveness seeks information about the situation and about how the other person feels. When you are responsive, you make yourself open to the other person's suggestions that you change your behavior. Actually, in an assertive-responsive transaction, both of you might make some alterations in the way you do things in order to arrive at a solution both of you find acceptable.

Assume that you are about to join a number of co-workers in a meeting with Personnel to discuss one of their policies that has been causing a problem. You would like support in challenging this policy. Before the meeting, you drop into a colleague's office to have the following conversation:

You: I wanted to chat with you before the meeting about this matter. Have you had any problem with it?
Him: No, not really.

> *You:* Well, here's the problem I had. A few months ago, Ted Wilson, who works for me, asked whether he could transfer to branch auditing. His children are grown, and he said he'd like to do some traveling. I hated to lose him, but he's worked well for me for years, and I wasn't going to give him a hassle. Then I found that if he did transfer and it didn't work out, he'd get terminated. I said, Hey, I want him back. No way, Personnel said. Out he goes, after fifteen years. I don't think it's right. In fact, it made me a bit angry.
>
> *Him:* Are you sure? You couldn't get him back under any circumstances?
>
> *You:* It would be as if he'd never worked here all those years. Doesn't that strike you as ridiculous?
>
> *Him:* It's hard to understand why that is.
>
> *You:* Then you're not happy with that policy.
>
> *Him:* Well, I haven't really thought it through, but off the top of my head . . .
>
> *You:* I'm going to make a strong argument that the policy be changed. Would you give me some support?
>
> *Him:* I hadn't thought about it.
>
> *You:* What would you need to give me support?

Just as a salesperson asks, "What has to happen for us to do business?" you ask your colleague what he needs in order to support you. You have taken an assertive-responsive approach. Suppose his reply is, "Well, I guess

I'd want to hear Personnel's side of it." You might come back with, "Of course. And if their explanation is essentially the same as mine, and you feel the way you do with me, would you give me your support?" If the other manager says, "Yes," then you have a commitment, something you probably would not have had if you'd employed only the assertive approach.

You will see other advantages of using the assertive-responsive approach throughout this book. It can assist you in getting help and commitments from everyone with whom you have to work—the employee with a performance problem, the peer with whom you need to collaborate or resolve a conflict, your boss who has been putting a lot of pressure on you or with whom you have a disagreement. The reason you get commitments through the assertive-responsive approach is because you involve the other person in the search for a solution or an answer. You make the other person a partner in the transaction. He or she "owns" what comes out of the transaction just as you do.

7

THE DIFFERENCE
SENSITIVITY MAKES

Peter S. is a bright, ambitious manager whose career
has stalled. He joined his corporation about a dozen years
ago, bringing with him an impressive background in
marketing services. For a time he even ran his own
company. People who have worked with him describe
him as tough, manipulative, demanding, and somewhat
unyielding. Peter built a power base on his superior
marketing skills. When pressed or opposed by management, Peter's ploy was to throw up his hands and say,
"If you want to go that way, you can have my job. I don't
want to have to work under those conditions." Usually
management, fearful of losing Peter, would back down.
This was almost always true of Peter's immediate superior, whom Peter bullied both in private and in public. Those who were close to Peter occasionally heard
him say regarding his boss, "He doesn't know his behind from his elbow."

Peter had credibility. He could get results from
employees, with whom he was very autocratic in his

management style. He often outshouted his colleagues. He was, in the language of one of his peers, a "gutter fighter." He brawled verbally with everyone, and managed to intimidate many. He also made an enemy of a man in another division of the company, who was in Peter's view relatively harmless. Unfortunately, that man, to everyone's surprise, was appointed to replace Peter's old boss, who was kicked upstairs. The new boss did not intimidate easily, and now Peter describes himself as waiting out his retirement. His career progress has been halted.

In retrospect, it is surprising that Peter didn't anticipate the possibility of the old enemy moving upward. The man was known in the company as being very powerful and quite ambitious, and Peter's boss, the foil for his bullying, had been rumored to be on the skids.

Fred P. had managed to climb as high as Peter. Unlike Peter, Fred was urbane and polished. He manipulated people too, but in a less obvious way than Peter. He was bright, ambitious, and highly talented. He wanted his boss's job.

When Fred suspected that his boss, who was nearing retirement age, might be asked to move aside, Fred began planting the information in top management that he was ready and willing. Then Fred took a Christmas vacation. When he came back, he learned that he had been fired. His boss had not been asked to take a less important position. He had been retained as too valuable to the organization and had agreed to stay on past normal retirement age. Fred paid a price for his indiscreet campaigning. He failed to anticipate the possibility—some in the organization said *probability*—that his boss would be solicited to stay on for a time.

Fred and Peter were caught short, miscalculating grievously. They had all, or almost all, the qualities of fast-track people. They had worked hard—and were smarter than most people. They looked and sounded like high potential people. They had solid professional skills. They had developed effective interpersonal skills, with higher management, peers, and subordinates.

Where did they fail? They lacked something vital, something that caused them to overlook some important developments or possibilities that could affect them. They missed some very meaningful clues. Both Fred and Peter lacked sensitivity.

Sensitivity may seem a strange term to use with regard to high potential, power-track people. It seems at odds with those commonly identifiable traits considered desirable in management, especially competitiveness and aggressiveness. Nevertheless sensitivity is the essential in many management activities, such as sizing up people, taking a reading of a situation, and understanding others' hidden agendas.

Most people fit within one of these three categories of sensitivity:

Sensitive people operate as open systems, interacting in healthy ways with others and within the organization. They are centered as opposed to self-centered and can respond to others without losing their sense of what and where they are. They can accord space to others as they themselves require it.

Insensitive people are self-centered and can't concern themselves with others, even when those others can affect their career advancement and power building. They erect psychological barriers that protect them from the feedback and perceptions of others. They do not want anything to disturb their self-image.

Hypersensitive people have inadequate boundaries to protect them from external influences. They react in the extreme to these influences. It is easy for them to lose their balance. They lack the toughness that is necessary for a realistic self-image.

Excessively self-centered and hypersensitive people have trouble staying on the fast or power track. The former miss the signs of change, or the negative feelings that others have toward them. The latter see them but fail to analyze them before they react. Neither is sufficiently rooted in reality to know what is happening around and to them. These are the people who often find themselves bypassed for promotions, shunted into harmless and powerless positions, or terminated. Whatever their fate, it usually comes as a nasty surprise to them.

If you want to have power, and keep it, you need to be tuned in to yourself. Your image of yourself has to be reasonably close to reality, that is, to how most people see you. It is important for you to know your limitations as well as your potentials and strengths. You must be as objective as possible.

Developing sensitivity to yourself is a continuing process. It means getting in touch with psychological needs, patterns, and tendencies. On the job, it involves finding out when and how you work best, when not to make decisions, what people and situations are upsetting, and what you need to learn and relearn.

Sensitive people take feedback from others very seriously, but with some caution. The self-centered person rejects feedback that is at variance with his or her self-image. Hypersensitive people usually have extreme reactions to any hints of faults. The balanced or centered person stops to consider whether the feedback is well founded.

By being able to encourage, receive, and evaluate feedback from others regarding their perceptions of you, you can not only help yourself get in better touch with your feelings, but win the respect and confidence of others. They will come to value you because you are self-confident, open, and trustworthy.

Sensitivity to the people around you is also essential, since being successful and powerful on the job requires knowing how you come across to them and what impact your behavior has on them. (They seldom volunteer the information.) You need an awareness of the people with whom you deal, in addition to being able to discern how they can help you up the ladder.

However, sensitivity on a one-to-one basis is not enough. You not only have to be tuned in to people, but to the events in their work group and the larger organizations of which they are a part, as well as their field, profession, and industry. Changes in these areas can alter work relationships and enhance your influence and power or threaten your authority and competence. You need to be sensitive, objective, and tough because you have to be aware of what changes—economic, technological, organizational—threaten your position and require you to make adjustments, some of which may be painful.

The sensitive person gets in the habit of testing his or her perceptions against reality as much as possible. It's not easy, because reality is subjective. So the best we can do is compare our perceptions against others'.

Besides being sensitive to yourself and others, it is important to be sensitive to what developments are occurring in your company and industry. People on the power track cannot afford to miss what is happening around them, since new developments may presage a change in the way they operate. The inability to see how your department or division will be affected by economic, business, or technological changes is an insufficiency that will sidetrack you. People who lose power, are shunted aside, or even terminated from responsible jobs will sometimes say afterward, "The signs were there; I should have recognized them."

You should become allied with a specific group of professionals or managers, ideally a group that has power and prestige. But you must not let your loyalty to a group blind you to the possibility that someday those people may be outside the power center, and you may have to cut yourself off and form new affiliations.

Develop a personal network inside and outside your organization. Through participation in clubs, trade and professional groups, seminars, conventions, trade shows, community and volunteer work, you should accumulate a list of people with whom you can trade information about the factors in your environment that represent potential or actual opportunities or dangers for you. If you have access to trade and professional groups, avail yourself of the knowledge and contacts they provide. You also need to be well read about developments in your industry and profession.

Within the company, a personal, informal network is invaluable. Most of the really important information about people, operations, decisions, and future developments is not available through formal channels.

Informal networks should be built carefully. You must recognize who have advance information and who are reasonably accurate in their analyses of developments. These are the people you want to cultivate. But remember, they are also interested in what you know, so you must be prepared to release some of your information. Organizational relationships are usually built on mutual advantage. (Specific recommendations on how to use the grapevine to your benefit will be dealt with in a later chapter.)

The further you go on the power or fast track, the better your exposure and visibility will be, and, most important, what and whom you know. Some mobile people turn their backs on their old cohorts and communication channels as they move up. Although it does not usually pay to remain closely identified with groups you have left behind lower in the hierarchy, you should never ignore the information and insights that some of your old associates can provide. The further up you go, the greater the sensitivity you must have to what is going on at all levels of your organization. Keep all your communication channels open.

At higher levels of the hierarchy there is a temptation to shut oneself off, to protect oneself, from information, presumably because if you keep yourself open, you'll hear things you would rather not hear. So-called executive suites that are separate from the rest of the company provide splendid isolation, and ignorance. In one company, a manager who was very skilled at using the grapevine occasionally reported more substantial— and sometimes worrisome—rumors to managers higher up. But after a time, he realized that he was causing them great anxiety, and that he himself was beginning to be regarded as a pariah.

The kill-the-messenger syndrome is usually very effective in making sure that management does not get the information that, no matter how painful, it desperately needs.

Sensitivity opens doors; it does not build barriers.

8

DRAWING POWER
FROM ABOVE

The nearest repository of power is, of course, your boss. This power is there for you, not for the taking, but for the giving. It's a lesson that Mark S. learned to his dismay. There were bad feelings between Mark's boss, Bill, and Bill's boss, Jerry. Jerry began to bypass Bill to talk with Mark directly. At first it was friendly talk, nothing to do with work. Then one day Jerry approached Mark with a job for him to do. Mark was uneasy, but Jerry assured him that he would later clear it with Bill. It bothered Mark to learn later that Jerry had not done so. Nevertheless the two established a friendly business relationship, and bypassing Bill became commonplace. Bill was understandably disturbed and grew quite frosty toward his subordinate.

At one crucial point, Bill submitted a proposal to Jerry outlining a merger with another department that he thought would create greater efficiency. Jerry brought the proposal to Mark, and told him why the proposal was a bad piece of work, although Jerry agreed that a merger should be considered. He asked Mark to re-write the proposal, and coached him in how it should be prepared. Mark had misgivings, but he trusted Jerry, so he went ahead with it.

Jerry presented Mark's version to higher management, letting it be known that Mark had authored it. Jerry also managed to circulate, informally, Bill's much-flawed proposal. Bill was furious, and Mark was embarrassed. But Jerry was grateful, telling Mark that Bill was on his way out.

Sure enough, within the month Bill's transfer to another division was announced. The announcement was laudatory, but everyone knew by then that it was involuntary and the new job had less status. Mark was shocked to learn that Bill's successor had been hired secretly from the outside. It had never been stated explicitly, but Mark had always assumed that he would be considered to replace Bill.

Relations between Jerry and Mark worsened. Mark's new boss, apparently aware of Mark's role in getting rid of Bill, was wary of his subordinate. He didn't trust Mark to be loyal. The longer Mark worked for his new boss, the more unhappy he became. Eventually he resigned.

Thanks to Jerry, Mark was able to take power from his boss. This power play was orchestrated by Jerry, but Mark didn't get to enjoy his illicit power. In fact, it caused his downfall.

Mark's situation has a historical parallel. General George Thomas, a great Union general of the Civil War, avoided this mistake. Early in the war, Thomas was urged to take certain actions and provide information that would undermine his boss, a general with suspected Southern sympathies. Thomas refused, citing his ethical responsibility to be loyal to his commanding general. He suffered for a time, but eventually achieved an enviable niche in American history as one of the greatest generals of the war. His reputation was never besmirched.

You may not be enthusiastic about your boss; you may see lots of opportunities to undermine him or her; you may even believe that your boss is an idiot. There may be people whispering in your ear that you have an obligation to the organization to help get rid of this inept person. Don't be fooled. If you do take such steps, you may find yourself regretting it. Right or wrong, smart or dumb, your boss is still your boss. The organization survives because of its managers. You will be seen as a negative, even destructive force. Furthermore, most people don't like conflicts and power plays. If you are responsible for one, you may get tagged as a troublemaker. In most cases you will not be regarded as a hero, no matter how inept your boss.

There is an unwritten commandment: Make your boss look good. This will be much appreciated. Your boss will like you, and other people will recognize you as a loyal subordinate.

What if nothing you can do will make the boss look good? For example, the boss is obsolete, stupid, incompetent, a drunk. Do you have to cover for him or her? It is considered good form to do so up to a point. You will be doing your part as long as you don't advertise what everyone probably already knows. Take over whatever responsibilities you have to, if your boss is unable to do them. Generally though, you should get your boss's okay for whatever authority you assume.

There are ways to do this without creating too much of a threat to your boss. If you act discreetly, you'll not only get a share of the boss's action, but his or her thanks as well. Since people elsewhere in the organization will know the difficulties you operate under, they'll be grateful, too. In time, they'll either remove the boss or find another place for you.

Keep in mind that the boss is there for a reason. You may not like or respect your manager, but it's likely that someone in higher management does. It may be because of past accomplishments that your boss has a position for which he or she is no longer suited. Perhaps management just doesn't want to take action that is painful, even though it is necessary.

The answer for you is to become what Eugene E. Jennings, author of *The Mobile Manager*, calls a *crucial subordinate*. Move into vacuums; take over jobs that are not being done well. In some cases, you'll obtain a lot of power this way. People will begin to say that you are actually running the department instead of old Fogbottom. In other cases, if your boss is on the power track, you'll move rapidly with him or her. In effect, you have a contract with your boss: I will make you look good, if you do good for me. The contract doesn't have to be explicit; it probably won't be. But chances are that both parties will understand that it is there, and will abide by it.

There are two cautions that need to be given here. The first is to be aware that while you need to be competent—it's a sine qua non of making a boss look good— you may become so expert, so skillful and knowledgeable that you become a threat to the boss. All managers are not wise enough to say, "Jamie knows more about the subject than I do," and cheerfully use Jamie as a resource (reflecting well on the manager who made it possible for good old Jamie to advance as far as he had). For a time you may be reasonably content hiding your light, but after a while it becomes burdensome and self-defeating. This may be the time to move on. The boss who feels threatened very often resorts to putting you down or finding some way to keep you on a short leash, and there's no reason to put up with that.

The other caution is to beware of what Jennings labels a shelfsitter, the boss who has gone as far as he or she will go. If that shelfsitter is blocking you, you won't succeed your boss in that position on the shelf, and you may not be able to get around the boss either, although in a few cases managers are promoted over a stationary boss. It will be necessary for you to make contacts throughout the organization, so when you decide to go out the window, you have a net there.

After you've been in a job for two or three years, you will have mastered about 80 percent. After that you'll only be picking up the other 20 percent, you'll be over-learning. So at that time, you have to make a critical decision. Will you stay on for a little longer in the hope that the boss will get bored and step aside, will you try to make a lateral move in your organization, or will you bail out altogether and go elsewhere?

If you stay beyond a certain time, after you have sufficiently demonstrated your competence and have stopped making progress on a substantial scale, you will begin to see your power erode. So, if you are stuck, set a time limit for getting unstuck. Otherwise you may wind up being known as Fogbottom's boy (or girl), and since Fogbottom probably has no power, neither will you.

BECOMING A CRUCIAL SUBORDINATE

One of the best opportunities for getting on a good footing with your boss is when he or she is new. You've been in the department; you know it. You may be one of several managers or supervisors reporting to the new boss, but you'd like primacy. Here are some suggestions to help you pursue a policy of enlightened self-interest, so you can be helpful without being too obvious.

Ease into the relationship. There is usually an introductory stage for the new manager from another location, agency, or company. He isn't in the learning stage yet, not really. He shakes a lot of hands and hears a lot of names, but impressions are blurred. During this stage you must respect the pressure he is under. Everyone is trying to impress him, and he probably feels boxed in. Don't try to load him with information or proposals for changes. Save your ammunition for when he is seriously studying the operation. That is when you want to become an important resource to him. Later, when he takes full charge of making decisions, he will regard you as someone he can trust to share some of his authority.

Schedule lunch. Some of your peers will probably wait for the boss to indicate he wants to have lunch with them, but don't assume that the new boss will extend invitations. He may not want to seem to single anyone out. He may however be happy to be asked. If you feel he might hesitate to join you alone, suggest a group luncheon. You'll be seen as a leader and organizer.

One advantage of talking with a new boss in an informal atmosphere is that you can more readily ask about his background and experience. The more you know about what he did and how he worked before joining your operation, the better you can anticipate his behavior and decisions later.

Look for personal help you can offer. A boss who has moved from a distance will probably appreciate any suggestions you can offer on services in the area—doctors, dentists, stores with good prices, plumbers, banks, places to see, and so forth. Your help may not have anything to do with the office, but it can establish you as a person who is as thoughtful as you are generous.

Solve your own problems. Uncertain about the new boss, others will probably run to him every time a problem arises to see how he wants it resolved. During the break-in period, this can amount to a real hassle. Demonstrate your competence by taking care of as many of your problems and making as many decisions as possible, then write him a short memo or make a verbal report of what you've done and why. That way you impress him with your ability and at the same time give him a chance to give you feedback on where he might differ with your approaches. However, be careful that you do not solve problems that truly belong only in his jurisdiction. Otherwise you will be seen as a threat.

Tell him about the people in your department. After he has had some time to get settled in his new assignment, prepare a rundown on the key personnel in your department. This can help the new boss learn what human resources are available. Remember that he has already seen the personnel files, so design the memo or report to update that information.

Ask your employees to describe the work in progress in a memo—who is doing what, why, and how far along the work is. This may be an appropriate time to forward suggestions and grievances from the people who report to you. It is certainly a legitimate way to call attention to you and your operation. But sell softly, it is better to submit a written report since he may want to defer any extensive discussion for a time.

Recommend the best role for him. When a new boss arrives on the scene, he may be unclear as to how he should handle the leadership transition. If the department is long established and if things are running fairly well, he may want to keep things as they are for a while.

On the other hand, if the department is demoralized and disorganized, if people are working at cross purposes, or if the department is filled with eager beavers who want to step up the pace, then a change of direction is indicated, and the sooner, the better.

Your recommendations to the new boss should be based on the needs of the department as you see them. But be sensitive to resistance. He may have priorities you don't know about. Don't put yourself at cross purposes with him by pushing your recommendations too hard.

Invite him to your meetings. The new boss may not be eager to participate in your conferences, but give him the opportunity. He may want the exposure. It is a good way for him to become comfortable with your coworkers, and for them to get used to him. You will probably want to set aside some time for him to talk about the problems he sees and his objectives. It will help your people see what kind of a person he is.

The danger in inviting your boss to your meetings is that he or she might be tempted to take over. Take some steps to maintain control.

1. *Tell the boss what role he is to play.* For example, tell him that there are some specific problems that you would like him to address. When you introduce him, let the people in the room know why he is there. Say that he will talk about those certain problems and answer some questions. This is a signal that he is not there to engage in a general discussion. If the boss's presence is needed for only a part of the meeting, let him know in advance how long he can expect to be there.

2. *Sit center stage.* If it's possible, take a chair at the head or the center of the table so it is clear that you are in charge of the meeting.

3. *Take charge from the outset.* Make the opening remarks or define the issues to be discussed. When his time is up, signal your boss that you want to move on. Thank him for his contribution and ask him whether he wants to sit in on the next item. Let him know that if he wants to leave, everyone will understand.

A meeting is a good way for your boss to see you apply your skills. It also provides the opportunity for you to strengthen your ties with him or her.

Actually, many of the recommendations described above for the new boss can work quite well in a continuing relationship. Even though you work with him or her on a daily basis, an occasional lunch or a drink after work fleshes out the relationship. In those less formal minutes, you can feel more comfortable saying things that you might not say in each other's office. Talking without an agenda is an important way of communicating.

You should give your boss periodic updates about the people who work for you. Nothing gives you more credibility and better public relations than the good work they do. They are your monuments, your chance to blow your own horn without ever mentioning your own name. If your subordinates are doing a great job, it means that you are, too.

You can make your relationship with your boss more important by giving feedback. In this way, you help your manager to define his or her most effective role in the department. Unless you have a boss who regards any negative feedback as warmly as a vial of plague bacteria, you might forge closer ties by telling to the boss what others in the department won't. No one likes to be seen as ineffective, and if you feel that your boss may be, you can find a way to say so. The boss may not like to hear it initially, but if you spare your manager the additional embarrassment of future mistakes, you will earn his gratitude, especially if you are the only one who dares or cares to give feedback.

When you give negative feedback, follow these suggestions:

Choose a time when the boss is receptive. The boss may create the situation by asking you, after he has made a decision or taken an action, what you think about it. Otherwise, select a time when you are alone with the boss (but not the men's room) when he doesn't seem harried or under time pressure.

Get his okay. "I have some thoughts about what you said to Greeley this morning in the meeting. Would you care to hear them?" Or, "Something's been bothering me about your assigning Glen to the Rockwell account. Can we discuss it?" Usually you will get a signal to go ahead.

Stick to facts and the boss's behavior. Talk about what you saw the boss do, or heard him say, that causes you concern. Don't get into attitude, hearsay, or motivation.

Follow up with evidence to support your opinion or judgment. Glen has made several important mistakes that have caused serious inconvenience for the department. Perhaps your boss was not aware of them in deciding on Glen for an important job. Greeley was noticeably crushed by how the boss spoke to him in the meeting. Several people in the department remarked later to you that they thought the boss was unkind. You know the boss doesn't deserve or want that kind of image.

If the boss gets defensive, a normal reaction, simply say, "I just wanted you to have this information. How you treat it is strictly up to you. But I did believe that you'd rather know it than not."

There are many areas where your boss does not get critical feedback from his or her boss, and it is impossible to be effective over the long term without knowing about your mistakes. As long as you deal with substantial issues, try to avoid speculation about motivation, stick with behavior observed, and present evidence to support your feedback, you are more likely than not to earn the boss's appreciation. There will come the time that the boss will want to show you memos or reports before they are finished to get your impression of them, talk with you about a decision, or check with you before taking action with an employee to see whether that action is appropriate.

You will have become the boss's confidante and trusted advisor. People will see you as having gained power from the boss.

You can find many other opportunities to play supportive and reinforcing roles for the boss. Although you don't want to be seen as a toady, giving positive feedback is perfectly legitimate. If you are a knowledgeable, trusted subordinate, no one can give better feedback than you. Here's how to support the boss without seeming to polish the apple:

Compliment the boss. There is nothing wrong with a compliment that is sincere and merited. When you've seen your boss make a sound move, say more than "That was good thinking." Ask, "What did you see in that situation that led you to do what you did?" or, "What would you have done if your approach hadn't worked?" Not only are you learning, but you are reinforcing the boss. You may think that the boss gets support and reinforcement from above, but you can't be sure of that. Any time the boss does something for you that you benefit from, let him or her know how much you appreciate it. Again, you are reinforcing the kind of behavior you would like to see repeated.

Listen actively. Sometimes your boss will use you as a sounding board. Don't just sit and nod, ask questions. If you don't understand something, ask the boss to clarify it. Once again, it is a learning experience for you, but it may also be for the boss. His or her new ideas or thinking may have some flaws or gaps that you can spot. This increases your boss's dependence on you. Remember that your power grows from such dependency.

Anticipate the boss's wishes. When you do your job in a way that wins your boss's approval, you are not apple polishing or being a toady. You are making both of you look good. One measure of your proficiency is the extent to which you can anticipate your boss's needs and expectations, and perform according to his or her standards.

Your reward, of course, is not only to get closer to the boss but to get more authority. Sometimes bosses are reluctant to delegate really challenging work and greater responsibility. Your first step may be to tell the boss that you would like a certain responsibility or assignment. Refer back to the chapter on persuasive power to refresh yourself on how to make a good sales presentation. After all, the transfer of power will benefit you, but the boss will be motivated to act if you show how it will benefit him or her.

If you can't get what you want from the direct approach, try one that is indirect:

Be *innovative*. Choose a task that is not an assigned responsibility of your reluctant delegator. If you fail, he won't worry that his head is on the block. If you succeed, the two of you can share the kudos. For example, training for new employees in the department has been delegated to section heads. The results are erratic, reflecting the style and the values of the current section chief. You would like to systematize the process. You mention to your boss that with the help of experienced people in the department, including the section chiefs, you could develop a training manual that would make the job easier and cut down on the time required. You get a go-ahead from the boss, because this is a no-lose situation for him. Once you develop the manual, it's an easy step to get put in charge of the training responsibility.

To take another example, you see a need for periodic productivity reports. Strictly speaking, the department can operate without them, but you sell the boss on the idea that feedback to the various employees would be beneficial to their work. The boss agrees to this, requiring only that your new project not interfere with your regular duties. You have now taken over management of an information resource. If your periodic feedback does indeed result in noticeable increases in productivity, you have grown in credibility. You have become a more crucial subordinate.

Develop a specialty. If you pick something your boss doesn't like to do or doesn't do well, you will be relieving a burden rather than invading someone's turf. To illustrate, there is continuing friction between your boss's department and Order Processing. She is not overly concerned with detail, and they are. You volunteer to work with Order Processing on ways to avoid the problems and the friction. To begin, you help to develop a new, simpler processing order form. Next thing you know, your boss is asking you to check her work. Soon you'll be indispensable. Or you might volunteer to do the periodic paperwork that Personnel requires. Your boss doesn't like to do it, but you are willing to because it helps you to carve out more authority for yourself.

Make it a partnership. This approach to persuading a reluctant delegator to let go of some responsibility is to try for a small piece of the action, even as a silent partner. Be prepared to leave most of the decisions to your boss and to let him take the credit. For example, your boss is hard at work designing a prototype. You mention that you have some ideas you think he'd like to consider. He does and incorporates some of them. In time, he may come to you and suggest you work on a project yourself—under minimal supervision. However, the boss will probably suggest it knowing that he will get the credit—and you have to be prepared to accept that.

Anytime you know that the boss is working on a project, even if it is only a report, and you have some ideas on the subject, offer your assistance. Each time the boss accepts and incorporates even one idea, you've contributed to building a closer relationship with him or her. In time, others in the department will recognize that the boss seems to invest a great deal of trust in you and your ideas.

There is one other way that people manage to get more responsibility, but it is risky. Say that your boss is away from the office, ill, or on a vacation or business trip. Something comes up that needs a decision. In your view it is not desirable to postpone the decision until the boss returns, so you accept the responsibility and make the decision. When the boss comes back, you are prepared to explain your decision. If the boss accepts that you were the best person to make such a decision, and that under the circumstances you made the best one you could, you may find that in the future when the boss leaves the office you will be charged with looking after certain things in the boss's absence. But if the boss feels that you should not have moved or that the decision was not the best, you have to be prepared to accept some negative feedback (and some negative feelings) as well as an erosion in your power base.

There may also be times when the boss delegates too much responsibility to you. This can be a signal that the boss regards you as crucial; however, it can also look to others in the department like you are allowing your boss to take advantage of you. This perception won't do your reputation any good, so you should take steps to avoid it. Some suggestions:

Delegate to someone else. But tell your boss what you've done. The boss may have reasons for wanting you alone to do the job. Another benefit of delegating is that your boss gets the message that you're overloaded.

Accept assignments conditionally. Some questions you might ask when you get extra work: "When do you *absolutely* have to have this?" "Does this job take priority over the report you asked me to prepare for tomorrow?" "Will you be upset if you don't get this back by the first of the week? I don't see how I can start on this until then."

Ignore some of the assignments until the boss mentions them. This may annoy your boss, but it will call attention to your plight. Reserve this for an extreme situation, after you've tried the other options and found that they didn't work.

USING INFORMATION
TO SCORE POINTS

In the business world, information is gold. No boss ever has enough of it. Most information they get from subordinates is about trouble or problems. No doubt they'd like to be on the receiving end of something positive, unthreatening, or neutral now and then. If you're looking for ways to increase your visibility and your influence with the boss, consider sending some of the following information.

Copies of memos. Managers usually consider showing the boss copies of memos sent to people outside the department, but they forget that that he may be equally interested in memos to people within the department, especially if they are complimentary or discuss an unusual task, project, or achievement. A copy of such a memo does two things: It gives the employee additional recognition, and it links your name to successful, out-of-the-ordinary action.

Employee comments and suggestions. Some managers relay verbal suggestions from employees to the boss. You'll get better mileage however by suggesting that the boss write a memo to be forwarded up the line. That way you can offer your solutions to problems raised by the employees and comment on their suggestions in a covering note. Your covering the memo with your own comments gives exposure to both you and the employee. In time you'll also earn the reputation as being manager of a creative department.

Articles. Usually the boss sends articles from magazines and newspapers to subordinates, but there is no reason why you can't send something you find interesting to your boss. The reading matter doesn't even have to be work related. Why not put your knowledge of the boss's outside or professional interests to work?

Of course, you want to be selective when it comes to sending articles that are not work related. You hardly want your boss to wonder where you find the time to do all the extracurricular reading.

Departmental round-up. Periodically you might prepare a memo for your employees, an abbreviated newsletter, that talks about who is working on what, recent achievements, future plans. Naturally a copy goes to the boss. If management walk through your area, use a bulletin board to spread the good news. Post memos from others that reflect favorably on your operation, complimentary letters from customers and clients, and newspaper clippings about any accomplishments of people in the department.

It doesn't pay to be too quietly efficient in your work. Let your boss know from time to time that your operation is running quite well. Keeping your people publicized tells them that you care about their welfare and work. It also adds to their confidence in you by showing them that you won't let your work group drift into the backwaters or be overlooked by higher management.

Keeping your boss informed is especially important if relations between you are strained, if you have a Theory X ("People must be coerced to work") or autocratic boss, or if your boss is physically removed from your location. You may be tempted to reduce your contacts, but that can only increase animosity, suspicion, and distance between you. When there are differences or distance involved, step up your contacts, even if it makes you uncomfortable. Let the boss know what you are doing or planning to do.

Also keep your boss informed about what you know. However, if you have access to higher-level people who are not in your boss's information network, don't emphasize your sources and your independent channels of communication. That information can be threatening. Some managers don't realize this. One manager told me that he would go to his boss with some juicy information and as soon as she heard it she would say, "How did you find that out?" or "Who told you that?" It finally dawned on him that she resented his knowing something she did not. So instead of saying, "So-and-so told me . . ." you might try, "Putting two and two together, it occurred to me that . . ."

If your boss is sparing of the information he or she passes along to you, you may consider taking the following steps to encourage more sharing:

Ask for advice instead of information. Information is rightly regarded as power; advice is another matter. Tight-lipped bosses hold on to information until the moment of greatest advantage, so it may be withheld as long as there is no advantage to releasing it. Advice can be seen as obligatory, that is, not only does giving advice not erode the boss's power, but it is an essential part of the boss's job in guiding subordinates. Rather than ask if the rumor about the staff cut is true, assume that there is truth in it: "I'm concerned about the possibility of a staff cut, and I've been planning, just in case, but I'd like your thinking on some problems that I think might arise, if and when a cut actually occurs."

Question indirectly. "Is it true that Ted's project is going to be terminated?" If you ask this way, you probably won't get a straight answer. You've been picking up clues that the project might not be as important to management as it once was. You suspect that overall plans have changed and that Ted's project no longer fits in, but your boss is not telling you anything. Try this approach: "Ted tells me that his typing load is more than his people can carry at the moment because of the project. I think he was going to suggest that I lend him some help. Would you recommend that I make some contingency plans to do so?"

Play to the boss's ego. One of your newer and best people is worried about being let go because of a rumored personnel cutback. If you ask your boss about it directly, you may get no answer. Include some flattery of your boss: "Emily is working very hard. It certainly confirms your feeling that she's a winner. But I understand she's worried about being axed. Last in, first out. I'm worried that it's getting in the way of her work. How do you think I ought to handle it?" You also suggest that although the boss was instrumental in hiring her, you are prepared to do the dirty work, if you must.

Be assuming. If you have a strong suspicion that you want confirmed, go to your boss and report it as something you've heard: "Rumors are flying that we're going to get a new vice president, and that Ed Joyce is getting the job." If it's not true, you'll get a denial. If it's true, you may still get a denial, although a flat-out denial might later suggest that your boss wasn't in the know. Chances are, if it's true, you'll get an ambiguous answer, or a stall ("I can't talk about it now"). Either one will tell you that there is probably substance to your suspicion.

If you are so successful, so competent, so informed as to make your boss think you are a threat, then you'll want to take the following steps to reassure him or her (when the boss is feeling threatened, your power is at stake):

Inform your boss about what you are doing and planning. Sound familiar? It should. It is prime advice. Your boss, whether the two of you are close personally or not, is a prime resource.

Don't blow your own horn. In talking about what you are doing, you'll naturally want to talk about significant accomplishments, but in so doing, concentrate on the results and skip the part about how brilliant you were in bringing them off. Treat your achievements as matter-of-factly as possible. You can't hide your competence, but you can avoid rubbing the boss's nose in it.

Soft-pedal criticism and disagreement, especially when others are looking on. Instead, look for things you can praise or agree with in your boss's actions or decisions. If you feel you must express misgivings about something, do so in private and in a low-key way: "I've been thinking about our discussion this morning, and there's something I thought I should check with you about."

Consult on your decisions. This is one of the best ways to reaffirm your subordination and convey deference. You may have already made a decision, but you can let the boss know you value his or her thinking. If the boss disagrees with your line of thinking, be prepared to defend your stand or to modify it in accordance with the boss's thinking. If you don't want to take that risk, consult only on those issues on which you are still undecided or in areas where you believe you know the boss's thinking.

Let the boss know you appreciate the help. Even if it was minor, let the boss know you are grateful. You may have done most of the work on your own, but you can turn that into a pleasing plus for the boss: "You've given me the chance to do what I think best, and I want you to know that I appreciate it."

Watch what you say behind the boss's back. You can be sure that if you are critical or mocking, the word will get back, especially if you are considered a threat. Don't give anyone a chance to quote you. If you can't say anything positive, keep your mouth shut. People will come to realize that you are competent and growing in power. If the talk turns critical of your boss, change the subject. You may be tempted to have some fun at your boss's expense, but you'll wind up paying the bill.

It often takes so little to dampen your boss's fears about you and your ambition. The less your boss knows about what you're up to, the greater his or her anxiety.

The more the boss knows, the less reason to fear that you are engaging in all sorts of devious power plays. Nevertheless, if you cannot overcome the paranoia, and if the boss isn't likely to be moving, look for another meadow to graze in.

WORKING WITH THE BOSS WHO DRINKS

The boss who has a drinking problem presents a special challenge to you—and an exceptional opportunity. Chances are you'll have to do some covering for the alcoholic or the problem drinker, and that opens up the way for you to accumulate power. The more dependent the boss is on you, the more powerful you become. The boss may also come to resent you, which may be made worse by the personality changes that occur when someone has been drinking—irritability, paranoia, hostility.

The questions for you are these: How do you stay effective with a boss who has a problem that affects the job and how do you accumulate power from the drinker without incurring painful hostility that will impede you? Some recommendations:

Work with the pattern. In those matters that you must have the boss's okay or cooperation, watch for times when the boss is not debilitated from alcohol. Some drinking managers start at noon, and it is almost impossible to do business with them in the afternoon, some drink steadily, but are less debilitated first thing in the morning, others may go on binges and are unpredictable. To the best of your ability, work closest with the boss when he or she is least inebriated. If the boss insists on making important decisions when drunk, find a way to doublecheck the decision when his or her mind clears. On matters that will recur, try to get a policy statement when the boss is relatively sober that will permit you to operate on your own when the boss cannot. The more of these standing decisions you can pin down, the more effective you will be even though you labor under a severe burden. Of course, if you wind up with nearly carte blanche, the burden will not be so heavy. You'll gradually accumulate a great deal of power.

Don't get too closely associated with the drinking boss. Most heavy imbibers like company. You may find yourself receiving frequent invitations to lunch or for an afternoon break or happy hour. Should you accept? Yes, to be diplomatic you should occasionally go with the boss for lunch or happy hour. Lunch is preferable because you can leave without offending an inebriated boss who wants to go on drinking.

If you have lunch occasionally, you'll not only get on better terms with the boss, you'll often hear things you might not otherwise. Alcohol loosens the tongue. Unfortunately these experiences are not always positive. You may get some feedback on yourself that is inappropriate. After all, in that state the boss is in no position to give you measured feedback. Don't quarrel, and don't laugh it off. When you get a chance, change the subject. If you hear nasty gossip about someone else, don't forget the boss may regret the indiscretion later.

Thus, drinking with a drinking boss is a mixed bag. Take the good with the bad. Even the nasty feedback about you can be important. As exaggerated as it might be, there is probably a core of truth to the unpleasantness. You are less likely to have illusions about your real relationship with your boss if you take some of the nastiness seriously. As for the scurrilous gossip, file it away. Don't broadcast it. People will trace it back to your boss and create even more unpleasantness between you.

Don't get emotionally involved. Don't offer counsel. Try not to agonize over the boss's affliction. It is self-inflicted, remember. You have your own responsibilities. Don't waste your sympathy on the hard-drinking boss; it will not do either of you any good, but do look for opportunities to build your power.

Don't cover for the boss. Others in the organization probably know about the drinking. Don't try to pretend in public that there is no problem. Covering for an alcoholic can be an endless and frustrating job for which you will gain nothing. If the boss comes back from a liquid lunch or is on a bender, try to keep him or her out of the work activity. It's difficult to do, but try to persuade the boss to go home or at least close the office door and try to sleep it off. Just do what needs to be done. Eventually everyone will know who is running the operation.

Expand your authority when the boss is drinking. In addition to those responsibilities the boss delegates to you when he or she is relatively sober, look for opportunities to expand your power when the boss is not competent. Start small. Make decisions of relatively little importance, then check with the boss later to make sure he or she approves. Gradually and slowly increase the work you can undertake without checking with the intoxicated manager. You run a risk, no doubt about it.

You may make the boss feel threatened and anxious. On the other hand, you may enjoy the benefits of an unspoken bargain. The boss, without saying anything, will be grateful that you are keeping things going.

Time your departure. You may suffer the delusion that you can run the kingdom while the king is indisposed. But the king still has title and much of the power. Your power is borrowed. Furthermore, you may become so good at being a stand-in that management decides not to disturb a good arrangement. So when you have learned all there is to learn—or most of it—plot your course elsewhere.

COLLABORATION, NOT COMPETITION

For many people on the power track, the ideal boss-subordinate relationship is collaborative. Both boss and subordinate recognize that they are engaged in a partnership. Each needs the other. The manager assumes the role of director, coordinator, teacher, watching over the day-to-day responsibilities of the subordinate and providing opportunities for the subordinate to actualize his or her potential. The collaborative manager sets standards of performance that the subordinate is expected to observe. With the junior partner the manager establishes goals, giving the subordinate a clear sense of direction. As the subordinate masters a skill and achieves a goal, the manager helps the former to push his or her boundaries even more the next time. With collaborative, farsighted managers, subordinates grow, expand, and progress within the organization as their bosses/mentors do, gaining power at each step as the senior partners relinquish it.

Philip, who started out as group sales manager and went on to become chairman of the board of his large life insurance company, was just such a collaborative manager. When you joined his department as a trainee, you were told the following: "You are here to learn as much as you can as fast as you can. Wherever you see an opportunity to learn something, take it. If that opportunity is in my office, walk in. If you see someone else come into my office, you follow. If for some reason I don't want you there, I'll shake my head. Otherwise take a seat and listen to what is going on." When Philip retired from the chairmanship a few years ago, it is small wonder that he left his former trainees and assistants in responsible positions throughout the corporation.

If you are lucky enough to work for a Philip, you can look forward to a fast trip on the power track, if your manager deems you worthy of it. But most people find their relationships with their managers quite different. They dare not wait for their managers to see the need to grant them power; they might have to wait forever. They have to be shrewd in persuading their bosses to let go of power little by little, or they simply find opportunities to grab some power from time to time. In either case, the subordinates must take the initiative. They must take the first steps to expand their boundaries, to take on more responsibilities, and to acquire more power. For them, it is a matter of learning as much as they can, giving loyalty, being patient (but not too patient), and moving on when the dividends from their continuing investment grow disproportionately small.

Some power seekers' relationships with their bosses are competitive, unfortunately. The boss never stops seeing them as a threat. For them, it is sink or swim, which can be effective in sharpening and hardening their instincts, if they don't drown first.

Sometimes the power seeker becomes so hardened and so hungry for power that he or she tries to get rid of the boss by playing power games, manipulating, or bypassing the boss, becoming what Michael Maccoby in his famous book *The Gamesman* calls a jungle fighter. Ironically the jungle fighter may actually be applauded by the boss's bosses, who like to see a good scrap. They enjoy the coliseum. They don't mind a bit of blood, especially if it is that of someone they don't especially admire. But when the jungle fighter has destroyed the prey, the unfortunate boss, and looks around for greater opportunity within the organization, paths are often blocked by other beasts who have banded together. They might have enjoyed the spectacle from a distance, but who wants a bloody jungle fighter in his or her own part of the forest?

9

FOLLOWING THE
POWER TRACK

The power track continues upward, beyond your immediate boss. In the usual bureaucratic, hierarchical, pyramidal structure, the higher up, the more power. Cultivating your boss is an important first step, but it is only the first. There is an immense power reservoir above to tap, but the sluice gates are guarded carefully. In fact, the bureaucracy is set up to keep as little power from flowing downward as possible without crippling the function of the organization. You have identified the centers of power, the guardians of the sluice gates. Now that you know who they are, you want to make sure they know you.

The easiest way is socially. When you pass them in a corridor or in a conference room, greet them by name. It is simple, but many people don't do it. The smart people do. Years later, I still remember Linda N. She was an administrative assistant in a company where I worked. Within a few weeks of being hired, Linda knew the name of every important person on the staff, and she used their names each time she met them in the hallway or in the coffee room. After a short time everyone knew her name, too. How could you not be curious to know this attractive young woman who used your name and flashed such a warm smile? She provided such a contrast to all the faceless people who passed you head down or with a weak and forgettable "Hi."

If you are new, or if you haven't met some of the power people, be ready to introduce yourself. You don't have to make a big production. Just say something like, "I've been wanting to introduce myself, I'm George Martin, and I work with Jerry Landauer." That's all. Thereafter, when you see the person, use his or her name and flash a smile. Don't be discouraged if the person greets you impersonally, without using your name. Sometimes it's forgetfulness, other times it is a ploy to let you know that he or she is more important than you. If the person is worth knowing and being known by, continue to greet him or her warmly. After a time, most people come around and respond.

When you feel that you have established a rapport with one of these power people, you may want to stop for a brief chat when you meet. At first, make it brief and casual, especially if you are in an elevator. (You don't want them to resent you for having trapped them.) Do they like sports? Talk about a game the night before. Are they art buffs? You can mention an exhibit. Are they on the board of the symphony? Did they give a speech a few days before? Do your homework, but don't come on too strong. "I've heard some very complimentary remarks about your speech the other night before the chamber of commerce." "Did you see the review of last night's concert in the paper this morning?" People are usually very flattered that you have taken the trouble to learn what interests them and then to refer to those interests. But again, do not make too much of a fuss or seem sycophantic. You will destroy your chances of building a relationship. People in power tend to ask themselves, "What does he want?" If you are graceful and light, they will worry less. They'll just think you are an unusually nice and thoughtful person, which is exactly what you want them to think.

Be wary of talking departmental or organizational business when you meet the power people accidentally or casually. Some of them disapprove strongly of people bypassing the chain of command. If you have a request or an observation, these people believe you should go through the chain of command. An extreme example of this occurred in my younger days at a company where I worked. The occasion was a Christmas party, an event full of traps for the unwary. I was standing at the bar with an attractive, bright, and sometimes acerbic colleague when the chairman of the board engaged us in conversation. At first it was nothing serious. The party ended, the bar closed down, and the chairman invited the two of us downstairs to the hotel bar to continue the drinking and the talking. Then the talk turned more serious, and my colleague, fortified by alcohol, began to tell the chairman about the many problems the company was generating for itself at certain levels. The chairman grew very uncomfortable. I simply said, "It's true, and I'll document it in a memo." (I don't, however, recommend writing such memos.)

I did write the memo, disregarding the risk because I felt very secure in my job in those days. (Probably no one is that secure these days.) A day or so later, the chairman ran into me in the men's room. Obviously uncomfortable, he checked the stalls to make sure they were empty, then whispered to me that he had received the memo and his assistant would be in touch with me shortly. All that came of the adventure was that I established a good relationship with the assistant, who had a great deal of power. But I took a risk, because I might very well have offended the chairman, who was strictly a chain-of-command person. My tactic could have backfired.

A footnote: The chairman was right to check the stalls. Years later, I made an indiscreet remark about company practice to a co-worker in the men's room. Imagine my chagrin when out of one of the stalls walked this same chairman.

So much has been written about the dangers of mixing with power people at parties where alcohol is served. It seems unnecessary for me to deal with the subject at great length here. Suffice it for me to recall that shortly after a colleague had been promoted to a level higher than mine, I spoke to him at a celebration party in a denigrating way. I was very angry with him for what I thought was a deception on his part. Alcohol made me less selective of the words I used than had I been strictly sober. Later that colleague became my boss and eventually had the great pleasure of asking for my resignation.

SELLING UP THE LINE

If you want to make a large expenditure, to expand, or start a substantial project, it usually requires a decision that is made at a level higher than your boss. You can get a lot of good PR by sending ideas, suggestions, and proposals up the line like this. However, since the decision making is removed from you, you have very little control over it. You even have trouble finding out what, if anything, is happening to your idea. You can ask your boss, but odds are he or she won't know much more than you. Consider these steps:

Suggest to your boss that a meeting be arranged. It is best, of course, to make the presentation to the decision makers yourself. There is always something "lost in the translation" when someone else speaks for you. Your boss may be relieved not to have to do the talking. If you can't get a commitment to present your proposal yourself, seek permission to attend the meeting as a resource, to be there in case questions come up or there is a need for further information.

Offer to write a memo to the decision makers. If you can't attend the meeting, this step can be helpful. A memo can be ignored or get buried, but at least it gives you a chance to express your thinking in your own words. Conclude with an offer to talk with anyone who wishes more information, and you may be invited to the meeting after all.

Ask to talk with your boss's boss. Tactfully suggest that the three of you sit down to discuss your proposal. This may win you two partisans.

In any of your suggestions to participate actively on a level above your boss, you must take his or her feelings into consideration. The boss may not feel that any help is needed, or on the other hand, could be relieved that you want to do the detail work.

If you have reason to believe that your idea has stalled, or been tabled, try to come up with a new slant or benefit. You don't want to ask whether a decision has been made. You're inviting a "no." Either they have not decided or they see no reason to. You probably did not use up all your ammunition in the original proposal. There was probably at least one selling point you left out or covered incompletely, or perhaps there has been a new development, application or benefit that would constitute a door opener: "Here's something else that should be considered." Then go through the steps recommended previously to get a hearing.

As your idea goes up the line, it may get "improved." It is a fact of life within any organization that ideas belong to no one person, yet you would like to fight for the integrity of your plan and enhance your chances of getting credit for being innovative and imaginative.

If you push just so far, people will admire you for being a scrapper. You will also get more publicity, which can help you in pursuing the power track. If you push too far and too hard, you will alienate people who you'll have to work with in the future. You certainly don't want management reacting negatively to your next proposal.

How can you judge how strong a campaign you should wage to protect your idea or proposal? Here are some suggestions:

Get objective advice. You are probably too close to what is happening to think tactically. Ask for counsel from someone you respect, perhaps another manager who is experienced in the organization but not directly involved with what you are attempting. That person may be able to help you develop a perspective on your strengths and weaknesses, the pluses and minuses of your tactics. Then you can decide what course to pursue.

Many people do not take advantage of the objective viewpoints available to them. This is a mistake, especially for those involved in making an impression on people at a higher level in the organization. Others consult objective people to use as sounding boards, but disregard their analyses and recommendations if not what they want to hear. It is wise to consult, and even wiser to take seriously what is offered to you. That doesn't mean that you should always follow someone else's advice. It means that instead of rejecting advice because it doesn't suit you, stop yourself and ask why you have such a precipitate reaction.

Don't impute bad motives in public. If higher management is "fooling around" with your idea, don't assume they have impure or malicious motives. If you think they do, keep it to yourself. Assume that everyone, ally or not, is trying to operate in the best interests of the organization. Remember that your "superordinate" goal is to get your idea accepted with your name on it. Don't let your anger over someone's revisions or disagreement cause you to get sidetracked. When you are on the power track, you have to expect that people will take issue with you. In a later chapter, you'll find recommendations on how to handle opposition.

The term used above—superordinate goal—is one you should have engraved in your mind. It means that which is superior; it's the goal of goals. When you are on the power track, your superordinate goal is to build and keep power. You will be offered any number of opportunities to get thrown off course by quibbling, and fighting, but people who succeed are dominated by their superordinate goals. They never get thrown off course, or if they do they know how to get themselves back on quickly.

Refashion your ideas. If your original concept has been substantially altered, you may be able to come up with a second idea that embodies some aspects of the program that has been reshaped. If you can retain some of the idea and some of the credit, you've made substantial progress. If they hand you lemons . . . Remember your superordinate goal.

Find your bargaining advantage. Talk to whoever changed your recommendation. Find out what they are thinking. Support what you can and be as gracious as possible. They expect you to be defensive, so they will be too. If you aren't you will disarm them. They might even be willing to do you a favor in return for your support of their alterations. At any rate you'll probably win an IOU if you accept what they have done to your proposal and show that you harbor no negative feelings, only a desire to do what is best for the organization. If you feel angry and frustrated, hide it.

Put your arguments in writing. Reading the arguments for your original proposal may influence those who count more than your previous discussions did. But be careful, the letter's tone must be neutral. Stay away from impassioned pleas.

Before sending in your written comments, put them away for a day or two or show them to a trusted friend. Make sure that the heat of frustration didn't cause you to write anything that will come back to haunt you. You want your arguments to be as objective and dispassionate as possible. Even if you don't win this one, people will be impressed by the quality of your thinking and your articulateness.

Know when to give up. As the song that Kenny Rogers sings says, "Know when to hold 'em and know when to fold 'em." Once you have expressed your ideas in writing and got into the right hands, ease up. The key to effective action in campaigning for an idea or project is to know when to move on to something else. Otherwise, you will not only impair the chances of your idea (or its remnants) being accepted, but you may gain a reputation that will handicap you next time you have a proposal before higher management.

Consider yet another possibility. You've submitted an idea to higher management and been turned down. The form of the rejection is "Not now." You think persistence is needed. You are convinced that the idea is sound and has a chance of being accepted eventually. Why not now? You want to taste the sweet taste of success.

Persistence in the face of refusal is often viewed as admirable, even if it is unsuccessful. But there's a vital difference between seeming persistent and coming across as merely obstinate. You need to be certain you've got a good case. If you don't come back with good, new arguments for your idea, you may just look stubborn and unrealistic, a perception you can't afford. Some recommendations:

Present new information to disprove the major objection offered by the executives you are trying to convince. You don't want the decision makers to feel defensive, so emphasize that it was your oversight that caused the rejection: "I'm sorry I didn't have all these diagrams the first time, but as you can see, they show a way to build a conference room without disrupting floor traffic."

Ignore the objection. After allowing a day or two to go by, you may be able to revive your case by acting as if the objection had never been made. Rather than addressing yourself to it, you can simply present a list of new advantages that you overlooked on the first time around. For example, "I neglected to point out that training people to do two jobs would reduce our need for temporary help in the summer."

Minimize the objection if it's too important to ignore completely. What are the arguments that might reduce its weight? For example, "I admit that we could postpone resurfacing the delivery bays. But if you look at the way costs have gone up, it's safe to assume that we'll be paying 12 to 15 percent more to do the job next year, especially since the deterioration will be much greater than now."

Bring along a back up when you reopen your case. "Maggie told me about an experience she had that may shed some light on that security system I asked you to consider. Could I bring her by tomorrow to fill in?" When someone is willing to reinforce your point with a case history or statistical evidence, you gain a factual as well as a psychological boost for your argument.

Offer reassurance about the soundness of the move you're urging. When a higher executive asks for time to think over your proposal and you feel it's a stall that could last indefinitely, you may need to emphasize the wisdom of what you're encouraging. It could be that clearing up an uncertainty will do the trick: "The two companies I know of who have tried the system say they would never go back to their manual systems. We could check with them to see why they're so sold."

Ask for a face-to-face meeting. Presenting your new arguments in writing involves a risk because they are easier to ignore than an on-the-spot presentation. It's better to opt for an in-person session, where you can answer questions. So if you want to write a memo, use it as a follow-up to the face-to-face session.

Your skill, intelligence, and persistence in getting your ideas recognized up the line are vital if you are to attract the attention of key powerful people. You need the help and cooperation of your boss, which is why you should have a constructive, mutually beneficial working relationship. If you have a boss who is jealous or resentful of you to the extent of refusing to refer your proposals higher, then you have the alternatives of looking for a different boss or bypassing the present one to get sponsorship elsewhere.

It may happen during your career that you are saddled with a boss who has a bad reputation in the organization, and are afraid that his or her notoriety will rub off on you. You want to be taken seriously, and not be lumped together with someone who is considered abrasive, hard to get along with, insensitive, hard-driving, or unintelligent. You can help to separate yourself from your boss's negative reputation by following these suggestions.

Don't tolerate being lumped together with your boss. If others refer to "you people" or make remarks that appear to tie you closely with your boss, keep your cool, but ask them what they mean. Even if they pass it off as a joke, you will have given them the message that you are not be identified with your boss and that you expect to be dealt with as an individual.

Walk the line between attacking and defending. When you hear innuendoes about your boss, you don't have to take the defensive. All you have to say is, "Look, my boss gets results. We operate differently. We're both effective in our own ways." If you express disapproval, you may win some friends but if the word gets back you'll antagonize your boss.

Maintain your individuality in conversation. If you had a boss with whom you wanted to be closely identified, you would use the pronoun "we" as often as you could. In this case, use "I" as much as possible. Describe what you do and the way you do things in terms that will provide contrast between you and your boss. If everyone knows that your boss is an autocrat, talk about your democratic managerial style. People will get the message.

Cultivate friends and allies. The better you are known in the company and the more direct contacts you have, the less the chances that you will be affected by your boss's reputation.

Maintain freedom of operation. Even if your boss would like you to do things the way he or she does, if you are effective with your own style, you have a better chance of staying in control of your operation. The more successful you are at this, the more likely that you can remain your own person. No matter how big the boss's ego is, the bottom line figures are what count.

Remember that your boss is valued. Your boss keeps his or her job because of the value higher management places on him or her, so take care not to convey to them that you disagree with them. You don't want to appear disloyal, or to be questioning their judgment. However, management may know all about your boss's methods, and understand how difficult it must be to work for such a person. If you can get along with your boss while maintaining your integrity and independence, you will probably build considerable credit with management.

FINDING A MENTOR/SPONSOR

Although your relationship with your boss is important in your getting recognition elsewhere in the organization, it usually isn't enough. A few people are fortunate enough to work with strong, fast-moving, upwardly mobile bosses, and to move up as the boss does. But chances are, you have your own ambitions and your own ego. You want to go your own way and be your own person. You want to build your own power base, not just depend on associative power.

If you want to be your own person, you can benefit from contacts in other parts of management. But don't neglect your working relationship with your boss, and do keep up your competence. You will find that these two qualities, ability and loyalty, are what will bring you to the attention of others.

Much has been written in recent years about the value of having a sponsor, someone who endorses you when opportunities in the organization arise, and a mentor, in other words, a coach. Sometimes they are one and the same. If you are lucky it will be your boss, because when you have a mentor/sponsor who is above your boss in the hierarchy, you risk making your boss feel bypassed or insecure.

How do you attract the attention of a potential sponsor or mentor? By following many of the recommendations you have already read. Get to know who is who in the organization. Work to encourage them to know who you are. One of the best ways is to become so competent that word about you gets around, as it will. Another way is to send your ideas up the line, as I've described. Other recommendations are publicizing and promoting the welfare of your subordinates, and developing a reputation outside your company.

Are there more direct methods? Some people successfully make it a point to socialize with certain people of power at company outings and parties. They send notes of congratulation when power people achieve distinction, give a speech, or even write an exceptionally good memo for internal distribution. They ask for information from power people: "How would you advise a person who is interested in a career in marketing?" "What's the best way for a person to acquire management credentials?" "Considering where the company is going in the next five years, what advice would you give someone who would like to make tracks?"

Target your efforts. Review the recommendations in chapter four to determine where the power centers and people are. Who is in a position to do you the most good?

In many cases a sponsor/mentor will come to you. There are several reasons for this. The first reason involves ego. People feel flattered by protégés who listen to them and follow their counsel. The second reason is the chance to expand their influence. As you rise in the organization, you carry with you a certain loyalty to the people who've helped you. Third, your progress is affirmation of their worth and judgment. They picked a winner, and were able to help that winner with their knowledge, wisdom, and experience. Fourth, there is genuine concern for the organization. You can't let high potentials flounder, you need them to develop the overall strength of the company. Finally, there is the personal pleasure of seeing you get ahead. Your sponsor probably likes you, respects you, and wants good things for you.

The sponsor-protégé relationship is a very natural one, except when the relationship involves different sexes and threatens to become intimate. This is not recommended. If you are the junior partner in a sexual relationship, you may find your power increased with your sponsor, but others in the organization will do what they can to undermine your power in general.

Whether the relationship exists because you took the initiative or because a sponsor sought you out for your potential, your boss will probably feel threatened. You can't eliminate the threatened feelings entirely—after all, you are his or her subordinate and dealing with someone higher or outside—but you can lessen them. There are some recommendations to follow when your sponsor is not your immediate boss:

Maintain steady and frequent contact with your

boss. This is to assure your boss that you have not transferred your loyalties to someone else. You probably do feel loyal to your sponsor/mentor, but you must emphasize through your contacts with the boss that it does not interfere with the respect, loyalty, and good feelings you have for your manager. Remember, the minute you cut short communication with your boss, you encourage suspicion.

Don't talk with your sponsor about department business. If you do, it may get back to your boss, who'll suspect that you are working to undermine him or her. You'll build one relationship at the expense of another. Your boss can make your life miserable, so keep your conversations with your sponsor confined to the organization, the profession, the environment in which you work, you, or your progress, and leave your boss out of it.

Don't volunteer too much information about your relationship with your sponsor. You may be excited about the relationship and its benefits, but don't rub your boss's nose in it. If the boss tries to interrogate you, be discreet. Acknowledge that you do on occasion talk with your sponsor, that the two of you have a working friendship, and that you don't discuss your immediate work situation. The more matter-of-fact you are, the better your chance of convincing your boss that he or she shouldn't worry.

Don't let your relationship interfere with your responsibility. Spending long periods of work time away from your desk with your sponsor will not endear you to the boss or reassure your manager. Always remember that your boss can probably harm your record, or if not, your manager can find a hundred ways to make you miserable.

Let your boss know how much you value your relationship with him or her. Of course, only do this if it is true. Suppose, in your discussions with your mentor, you have discovered that you have an asset in a skill that you've learned on the job. "I'm beginning to understand," you say, "that I'm getting quite good at managing my time and schedule, and I realize how appreciative I should be toward you and all your prodding and encouraging me to get my work methods cleaned up." Or, "I seem to work at my best when I have control and freedom in my work, and I have you to thank for letting me work so much on my own." In short, find something good about your experience with your boss and give him or her feedback. Your manager needs to feel appreciated.

Ideally, your boss should recognize that the attention your sponsor/mentor pays you could reflect well on him or her, but that's not always the case. Some people never develop that kind of objectivity. As your power by association grows, your boss will probably respect it. If he or she doesn't, and seeks actually to "punish" you for having gone outside for help and guidance, it may be time to investigate what opportunities lie elsewhere, even if you have to make a lateral move.

Sometimes your boss will see your relationship with your sponsor/mentor as nothing special. One woman found this to be true when, after several years in the field as a salesperson, she came back to the home office to work on the marketing staff. From time to time while in the field, she had heard people talk about Ruth, a member of the marketing department and a well-respected economist. "Right away," she said, "I was impressed by Ruth's intelligence and the fact that she was her own person. I never was sure who she reported to, but she knew everyone and was in on everything." The young woman, Beth, began to spend much of her time with the older woman. They frequently conversed in the office, had lunch together, and occasionally had a drink or two after hours. "The woman knew everything about the company. She thrived on it. She told me who was important, who was worth knowing, or cultivating."

Beth benefited from Ruth's being invited to almost every meeting. Others valued her brightness, too. Gradually Ruth became Beth's mentor and sponsor. She obtained invitations for Beth occasionally to attend high level meetings. She talked freely about how much promise she felt her protégée to have. She even advised Beth on how to dress, what skills to sharpen or to acquire ("She insisted I take a workshop in presentation skills"), and how to present a proposal to management. "I went far pretty fast," says Beth, "and Ruth gets a lot of credit."

How did Beth's boss feel about it? "At first, he didn't like it. He'd try to warn me off by saying I shouldn't spend too much time with Ruth. Ruth had a lot of enemies. It's true, a lot of people didn't like her because she was smart and outspoken. But I thought it was worth the risk." Beth performed very conscientiously for her boss, built a close working relationship with him, and supported him in any way possible. Gradually he came to care very little that Beth was a close friend of Ruth.

Unfortunately, after a time, Beth ran into a problem that many protégés experience: Ruth was threatening to dominate her working life. The relationship between an up-and-coming person and a mentor satisfies a need in both, but eventually it is not surprising that one may derive less fulfillment than the other. Beth may appreciate Ruth's advice but not at the expense of her own ego. Changing the old relationship is not always easy. Beth doesn't need an enemy, and she doesn't want a sullen ex-friend. She wants Ruth to feel friendly, interested, involved in her progress, but not dominating or proprietary. Beth wants Ruth to remain someone who will actively be part of her network of high level, knowledgeable people—an advocate, a listening post, a sensor.

If you are in a position like Beth's, don't stop your contacts or conversations, just change their focus. For example:

Ask hypothetical or future-oriented questions. Tap the mentor's knowledge and experience in areas that are not threatening. Don't dwell on what you have done or what you are doing; it might draw analysis and criticism. Talk instead about what you might do: "One of my assistants has been pushing me to think more about direct-mail campaigns on Fabusol. Seems to me that you used to get good results with direct mail."

Changes are your sponsor/mentor will be off and running, and you'll probably learn a lot. Although you'll still be getting counsel, you won't have to commit yourself to following the advice or risk getting into an argument.

Talk about new developments in the company or

industry. Conversation starters such as, "I understand Mackey is running into problems on their Reeltape line," or "What do you think about our decision to take over Balltype?" will probably encourage a discussion that won't wind up in controversy. At the same time you'll be tapping a rich vein of knowledge.

Ask about your former mentor's new job. People like to display their expertise. You can provide the opportunity, and you don't have to be wary of what happens.

Following the above advice may to some extent perpetuate the old counseling role. However, it is likely that, at least for a while, your former sponsor/mentor will not see you as a bona fide equal. If you can accept that, you will find that he or she still has a lot to give— so you might as well take it and use it.

A HIGH LEVEL NETWORK

By advancing your ideas, proposals, and suggestions, being sociable and polite, asking people for advice and information, performing in an exemplary manner, and forging a close relationship with your boss, you can acquire both a solid reputation in the organization as someone who is worth knowing and watching, and a network of people who know and watch you. People like to be associated with winners. On the other hand, they also like to try to trip you up, if you are a winner who is a threat to them. It is for this reason that, earlier, I emphasized the importance, for achieving and maintaining power, of being sensitive to everyone and everything around you.

Nevertheless, if you can avoid all the obstacles, you can accumulate an important working network of high level people, power people who can come to your aid when you

> want a promotion or additional responsibility;
> need resources to do a particular job;
> are trying to sell a project;
> need allies in a political situation;
> need help in dispelling a threat to you.

Powerful people risk losing their power if they lose sight of the reality of their need for others. They sometimes forget that they have power because of those other people, who can take it away just as they gave it.

10

POWER FROM
THE PEOPLE

If you manage people, you have a double power base, first, because you manage resources—manufacturing, service, sales, technical, and so forth. The more essential your resource is to the organization's profits, the more power you could have, potentially. Secondly, your competence in managing that resource can be a source of power.

If you are to cultivate this power, you'll need help. You will need the collaboration of your subordinates. If you give them what they want and need, chances are excellent that they will reciprocate. You should view your relationship as a partnership, or a team effort.

Many managers on the power track focus their eyes upward. That is necessary, of course, but they overlook the tremendous resource they are managing. They often fail to understand how they can unlock the significant power that rests in a successful partnership between manager and subordinates. In a successful partnership your people perform effectively for you, helping you and the organization to reach the goals that are important to both of you. When you are successful, the record of achievement speaks for itself. But you'll also find that your employees will speak for you (and to you about what goes on elsewhere). They'll talk about how competent you are as a boss, how you make it possible for your people to do the kind of job they want to do and are capable of doing, how you create the kind of work environment in which people can grow and extend themselves, and how you can be trusted. In time, your peers and higher management will get the message that you know what you are doing, and that while you are interested in achieving short-term results, you are just as concerned about long-term development of the organization's human assets. Your reputation will grow, and with it, your power.

THE MANAGER AS MOTIVATOR

The principles of management by motivation are very simple to understand and easy to apply. It is, perhaps, for this reason that many managers distrust them, and are reluctant to practice them. You will see that they are worth consideration.

As a first step, take stock of your assumptions about people. You undoubtedly remember Douglas McGregor's Theory X that people have to be coerced into producing, that they don't really want to work, so you have to punish them to keep them in line. A lot of managers still believe that about most of the people who work for them. As a result, these managers are never able to develop their people into the kind of resource that gives them power.

The closer to Theory Y your assumptions about people are, the better able to cultivate your assets you will be. To refresh your memory, here's how McGregor describes Theory Y assumptions: Work is natural to people. They will commit themselves to objectives that are important to them, and the importance of these objectives depends on the rewards to be gained by achieving them. People seek responsibility and apply imagination and creativity to their work.

Theory Y assumptions are helpful to the manager because they help direct his or her energies most effectively. If you assume that your employees are ready and willing to do a good job for you, then you can see your job as enhancing rather than enforcing. You make it possible for them to work well for you. It is a lot easier to guide than to push.

Granted, there will always be reluctant, problem employees. You will run into an occasional person who, if given the choice, prefers play to work. However, you will find that this is not true of most people.

Frederick Herzberg's research is a useful supplement to Theory Y. Herzberg, in his two-factor theory of motivation, discovered the following to be motivators:

- *achievement,* the successful completion of a job or a task;
- *recognition,* an act of praise or some other notice of the achievement;
- *work itself,* tasks as sources of good feelings about the work done;

- *responsibility*, for one's own work or that of others, new tasks and assignments;
- *advancement*, an actual improvement in status and position;
- *possibility for growth*, potential to rise in the organization.

Consider the implications of Herzberg's widely accepted research. People can be narrated by the work they do, the achievements they accomplish, and recognition of those achievements. They want to grow and make progress, to improve their status.

Who is the key to all of these motivating factors? You, of course. You make work meaningful for your employees. When they do it well, you reward them. You make it possible for them to achieve, to improve their status (and you don't have to promote them to do this). Remember what McGregor said in his book, *The Human Side of Enterprise:* "Commitment to objectives is a function of the rewards associated with achievement of those objectives." You control many of the rewards that are available to employees.

Rewards, as McGregor points out, are a determinant in what choices people make. These choices range from minute to major. For example, you walk into a restaurant, pick up the menu, and decide what you'll have for lunch. The cheeseburger seems more delicious than broiled fish at the moment. Your reward for this choice will be a tasty cheeseburger. On another level, you decide whether you will stay in your present job with the organization you work for now or take the job offered by ABC company. The value of the reward is what in large part helps you decide. If you are a marketing person and love what you're doing, someone could offer you an insider financial job at half again the income you make in marketing to no avail. The satisfaction, the sense of achievement, the freedom, in short, the rewards you get from your marketing position are worth more than the additional money.

Rewards are only one determinant because in choosing a reward, you have to believe that you have a pretty good chance of getting it. For example, if you, the marketing person, would like to have the prestigious home office financial position with the substantial salary, but you worry about your ability to do the job, you'll decide to stay where you are because there you know you can gain your reward. You aren't so sure in the financial job. By the same token, even though you run five miles every morning, and the idea of winning the 27-mile marathon is of great value to you, you aren't likely to try it until you know you have a good chance of finishing the course.

What does all this mean to you as a manager? How can you gain power from understanding motivation theory? If you know how to enhance the motivating forces in people, if you can provide the rewards that are valuable to them, if you can increase their self-confidence on the job, then you are going to have a highly productive, committed, loyal group of people working for you, and that's a considerable source of power.

There are five steps you should follow to enhance the motivations of the people who report to you:

1. *Let them know what you expect them to do.* Many managers assume that employees, especially those who have been around for a while, understand what the manager expects of them—objectives, methods of doing the work, standards of performance, and so forth. But, you'd be wrong to assume that all of your people know precisely what kind of work you want done, how you want it done, what will happen as a result of its being done well, or why it should be done at all.

One of the best ways of letting people know what you want done and how is through setting goals. Set objectives with your people. Objectives are just as important to them as they are to you. They not only tell people where they are headed, but they allow a sense of achievement when they've gotten there. Talk about standards. "I want 200 units produced on a daily basis with a rejection rate of no more than 2 percent." "I expect you to turn in an average monthly volume of $15,000. You should make 15 calls on new customers each week."

People like to know what they are expected to do. Be as specific as you think desirable. However, once you set a goal, insist on it. If it is not reached, find out why. If you let it slide or simply dismiss it, people will not take the goals seriously, and you will lose credibility. If someone fails to reach a goal because of inadequate effort, insist that the person intensify his or her energies next time, otherwise you may have to consider probation or termination. If the goal proves to be unattainable, set a more realistic one. Just be sure that you account for each goal you set.

2. *Make the work valuable.* Every task, assignment, job, or responsibility should have a reward connected with it. Some people have powerful internal reward systems. When they work, they want to feel that they are growing (that they're better at doing the work this month than they were last, or that they've acquired new skills or knowledge), or they want more status, achievement, self-esteem, or peer approval and acceptance.

You can get a sense of what kinds of rewards people look for in their work, and then to the best of your ability, you can assign them the kinds of tasks, jobs, and work that will give them what they consider to be valuable. Remember that Herzberg says that people are motivated by the work itself. Thus the more meaningful the work, the greater the motivation to do it well.

Study the work history of your people. Talk to them about what they like in their work. You'll usually find a correlation between what people like to do and what they do well. Use this knowledge to make assignments and confer responsibilities.

You can reinforce your employees' internal rewards with your own external rewards. When people do well, recognize it. Herzberg's research also shows that people are motivated by recognition of achievement, which you can provide. The reward doesn't have to be elaborate. It can be money or a promotion, but if you can't offer either one, the following are suggestions for external rewards:

- more interesting or responsible work;
- training to help them develop new proficiency;
- more desirable workplace;

- publicity about their record or achievement;
- more freedom and control over their own work;
- better or newer equipment;
- career counseling;
- job rotation.

In addition, you have an inexhaustible supply of one of the most potent rewards or reinforcers in existence: praise. People never tire of it. You probably do not give as much of it as you think you do or should. If you praise specifically, that is, make it clear exactly what kind of performance you like, and if you practice praising consistently, you will encourage the repetition of the kind of behavior and performance you want on the job.

Through your rewards, especially praise, you actually help employees to shape their behavior so as to more effectively do the work you want them to do. Your department's message should always be: "Around here, when you do a good job, you get rewarded."

3. *Make the job feasible.* No matter how attractive a reward is, people aren't going to try for it unless they see a reasonable chance of getting it. So when you assign work, follow the steps below:

Define the task as precisely as possible. Think of what has to be done phase by phase. Also, explain what will happen as a result of the work, the goal. If you break down the job into stages, you'll help the employee to believe that the job can be done.

Set standards. Explain how the job is to be done. This may include what you consider to be minimally acceptable—24 units a day—or desirable—30 units. Standards should also include a time frame, you want the job done in three weeks, otherwise the employee may think you want it done in a week, which could make the task seem too difficult.

Describe the resources available. What authority, people, equipment, facilities, experts, and precedents or guidelines are available to help the employee complete the task? In addition you may want to provide special training, be a coach or collaborator, grant relief from other duties, or remove organizational barriers.

4. *Give feedback.* While employees are trying to do the job that you've assigned, tell them how they are doing. Employees frequently complain that they hear about it only when they've goofed or failed, not when they have done a good job. Whether the feedback is positive or negative, follow these steps:

Give feedback immediately. If there's been a mistake made, you want it corrected as quickly as possible. If there's been a good performance, you want its details fresh in the employee's mind so that he or she knows what to repeat.

Be specific. Describe in detail what went wrong or right. Don't just say, "You're not very conscientious," or "You're doing a good job, Keep it up." The employee needs specificity if he or she is to avoid or repeat the behavior.

Be consistent. When work is done exceptionally well, mention it. Don't let opportunities for praise and reinforcement pass. Don't delay criticism, because the employee needs that to learn to do the job well. No one wants to be a fumbler. Be sensitive to that.

5. *Reward the performance you want.* When the employee does what you expect him or her to do, reward, recognize, and reinforce. You'll stand a good

chance of getting more of the same. This will have long-range effects, since your employees will tell others that in your department they are appreciated.

Your employees can give you some of the PR you need within your organization. When they turn in consistently highly motivated, high quality performances, your peers and higher management will notice that you get consistently superior results. They may also note you as a power to be dealt with, but that is a risk you have to take.

COACHING FOR GROWTH

Coaching for growth means helping your subordinates to develop their potential, for you, for the organization, and for themselves. Most managers don't do this consistently. If you don't, you could be missing out on at least three important benefits:

1. Your assisting and guiding subordinates in increasing their effectiveness on the job, in expanding their knowledge, skills, and experience, has a motivational impact. Research in the behavioral sciences, such as Herzberg's, has clearly established that a prime motivator in most people is the desire to become better at what they do, to grow, and to progress in their work. Few people are satisfied to stand still, to stay the same year after year.

2. The second benefit in coaching for the long term is the development of resources that will later be valuable to you. After all, you constantly face new challenges defined by the economy, the marketplace, the laws and regulations, changing values of the work force, political developments, and the like. The conditions

under which you do your job will be different next year. This means you have to upgrade the ability of the people who report to you to meet those altered conditions and new challenges. They need your help and guidance in developing the skills necessary to achieve organizational objectives. Nothing erodes a manager's power more surely than an obsolescent work group.

3. Coaching long term has vital political implications and benefits for you. In the first place, you develop a strong department that could survive your leaving, in case the opportunity to move up came your way. A viable, functioning work group is a strength for you. Secondly, you bring people along who'll be allies when you need them. When you develop people who move out and up in the organization, your coaching of them is a missionary effort on your own behalf. They broadcast the message of your ability. When you need support, they are there to provide it or to solicit it for you.

To accomplish all three objectives, here are some recommendations to consider:

Schedule periodic coaching sessions. You should make coaching a calendar event. If you don't, you risk letting other responsibilities crowd this obligation out. Plan at least one long-term coaching session with each employee a year.

Ask for information. Ask your employees the same questions you ask yourself in plotting your career strategy:

- What aspects of your work do you like least? Most?
- What functions would you like to spend more time doing? Less?

- What kinds of tasks or responsibilities that you
  do not have would you like to have?
- What kinds of work and responsibilities do you
  see yourself having in three to five years?

Add your observations. Your own observations and records should show areas of achievement and patterns of successful behavior as well as weaknesses. You probably also have clues to what kinds of work employees show enthusiasm for and talent in performing.

Present specific guidelines. "Growth and development" is an amorphous phrase. Giving shape to a growth and development program is a job that requires managerial imagination. You should, in initial and subsequent discussions, point to such specific developmental experiences as further training and education, field trips, temporary duty in another department, stretching assignments, and reading. These suggestions should be part of the notes you take during sessions and file away for future guidance.

Provide opportunities to exercise and apply expanding capabilities. When you make work assignments, try not to give them automatically to people who have done well in the past. Consider who might grow the most by doing them. When you have tasks that have become "old hat" to some, let others take them on, others who might find them challenging.

Coaching is a continuing process. Do you coach as much as you should? Test yourself with the following questions:

- Do you take advantage of every chance to to
  provide a learning opportunity for a subordinate?

- Do you have a regular schedule for discussing with subordinates those skills and talents that can be developed for the future?
- Do you conscientiously try to maintain that schedule?
- Do you have in mind for your subordinates one or two experiences or assignments that could stretch each of them and contribute to his or her growth and development?
- Have you provided one or two developmental experiences for each subordinate during the past six months?

THE ART OF BEING A MENTOR

With one of your key or more promising people, consider going beyond coaching. Just as you'd seek out a mentor or sponsor, seek out one of your people who would benefit from your teaching and counseling. Being a mentor has practical advantages for you. You can

- strengthen your department by increasing the skills of key employees;
- groom a possible successor;
- earn a reputation of being someone who can spot and develop talent and potential for the organization;
- increase your influence in the organization as your protégés move throughout the organization;
- pave the way for your own success (a well-developed department and successors leave you the freedom to take on additional or different responsibilities when the opportunity arises).

If you are clear about your strengths, willing to share yourself with a less experienced employee, and can be candid about the ins and outs of organizational progress, you will be valued as a mentor. Some other important traits for a mentor include knowledge of the organization and people in it, respect of your peers, and acquaintance with the use of power.

There's no formality necessary to being a mentor—no classroom atmosphere, no structure—but there is a lot of time, effort, and concern involved. You will be a more successful mentor if you are willing to spend the time necessary to do a good job with a protégé, to set aside hours for counseling, in-depth discussions, to be available for consultation, and so forth.

Being a mentor also gives you access to other promising subordinates, who, perhaps feeling left out, will take steps to improve their performance and your opinion of them. They will make a bid to be your protégé.

Your success as a mentor will be considerably enhanced if you can continually raise the performance level and actualize the potential of your employees. The proficiency of your employees will attest to your own. Your evident ability to manage well will give you both status and power in the organization. In most organizations in the private and public sectors today, effective management is in short supply. You do not need to worry that you will not be noticed if you demonstrate your superiority in getting the results you want from the people you manage.

11

YOUR PEERS AND YOUR POWER

It's safe to say that many people—probably most—lack practical knowledge about power relationships and dynamics in organizations. I demonstrate this repeatedly in workshops in which I ask the participants to perform the following exercise:

> You are a department head who has been asked to lead a task force to study the adoption of flextime by your organization and to make recommendations for its design and administration. Your mandate has been given you by a vice president who has suggested that certain personnel be members of the task force. However, the actual recruiting has been left to you.
>
> You have little difficulty persuading other managers on your level to lend you key people for your part-time task force, which, you estimate, will require an average of four hours'

participation per week for several months. There is one prospective member, a statistical analyst, whom you want to recruit but whose boss has so far been reluctant to release him for the time you need. Your counterpart is in theory equal to you but, in fact, is highly regarded by management and considered by her other peers, including you, to be on the fast track. She has achieved high visibility and much autonomy in her department. You have already determined that you cannot put pressure on her to let her subordinate join your task force. You have just left her office after an indecisive discussion. She has told you that she will think about it, but she has also made it clear to you that she has in mind an elaborate project that will require much time from the subordinate whom you wish to recruit. You decide to write her a memo to try to sell her once more on the release of her analyst for your task force.

Most of the memos written by this exercise's participants fall into two categories. The first is the rather unimaginative wear-her-down approach, a repetition in writing of all the reasons why it would be good to release the subordinate. These memos can usually be dismissed with the question, "Why do you keep telling her what she already knows?" Apparently that is many people's idea of persuasion.

The second type of memo is more interesting and usually involves a not-so-subtle attempt at intimidation.

In spite of the exercise's directions' caution against applying pressure, many participants opt for doing just that. They threaten her, chiefly by suggesting that if she doesn't let go of the analyst, they will talk to the vice president about her refusal. They attempt to put the threat in diplomatic terms: "I'm sure the vice president will be very disappointed to hear . . ." Other participants are heavy-handed: They "copy" the memo to the vice president. But a threat is a threat, and these participants are often surprised when I tell them that they are about to have their heads handed to them. They are simply naïve about the realities of organizational power.

The participants who adopt the heavy-handed approach violate at least two rules involving power among peers. First, don't try to use power that you don't have, and second, don't use threats except as a last resort.

Let's examine the case carefully. You have the authority to form a task force, but its composition is up to you. Since the vice president has suggested certain people, you may legitimately use that fact in approaching the managers of these people. You must not assume, however, that the suggestion is a mandate that you can use. In fact, if you fail to negotiate the release of these people, the onus will probably be yours, and not the failure of the manager who declined to offer his or her subordinate. Thus, writing a memo with a copy to the vice president threatening your resistant colleague is an admission of your failure. It will backfire. Furthermore, your reluctant colleague's own clout with higher management suggests that she has the means for revenge in a power game.

Relatively few participants see the need to negotiate with their colleague. What benefits can they offer to get past her resistance? She obviously likes visibility, most power people do. So the performance of her key subordinate can reflect glory on her, and if you let it be known that she gave up her subordinate at expense to her of her own project, then you win more points for her.

Your colleague also likes control. This is evident from the way she controls the dynamics of the situation involving you and your task force. You can suggest that if she does not have a voice in the task force, she will lose some control. After all, the flextime system will affect her, whether she allows the participation of her subordinate or not.

Some participants shrewdly offer to lend one or more people to make up for her personnel lost to the project she wants to launch. This practically forces her into negotiation. If you adopt such a tactic, you are saying, "Here's my demonstration of good will. How about one from you?"

In most organizational situations and relationships, negotiation is the key to peer cooperation, and to building power bases with peers. The essence of negotiation is that people don't have to participate unless it benefits them. Negotiation with peers is worthwhile since they can help you to build a powerful base, and are useful to you in forming alliances, building collaboration, acting as mentors, sharing information, and offering support.

GAINING SUPPORT

When you go to a colleague and ask for support, if you have an idea that you would like seconded or endorsed, a change you'd like cooperation on, or a policy that you'd like to question, expect the possibility that, initially at least, you'll encounter some opposition. A few years ago, the Research Institute of America did a study in which they identified eight anxiety-producing factors that are most likely to increase others' resistance to change. Knowing these factors and anticipating the reactions they stimulate can go a long way toward helping you allay fears in those to whom you propose an idea or a project.

1. *Threat to security.* If your peer supports you, will it jeopardize his or her relationships with higher management, other coworkers? Will the support involve the person in an unpleasant conflict?

2. *Diminution of self-esteem.* Will the person's image of himself or herself be in any way diminished by granting you support? For example, could that support extend to an act of deception or damage to another's status and create discomfort in your ally?

3. *Diminution of status.* Will your ally risk looking less important than before? Will his or her status be reduced if things don't go right?

4. *Inconvenience.* What established routines might get upset by your proposal and others' support of it? Will the benefits of this support justify the disruption and change?

5. *Work and pressure.* Will your ally have to work harder or be subjected to greater pressure? Will the rewards for greater effort and stress be worth it?

6. *Environment.* How will the work and physical environments be changed for the better? What improvements can be reasonably assured?

7. *Human contact.* How will existing relationships fare? Will they be changed for the better—or for the

worse? What new relationships will be necessary? What are the implications for your supporters?

8. *Past experience.* What changes have your allies been subjected to before as a result of support they have given? Did results match promises? What in their relationships with you might cause them to hesitate?

When you go to a colleague for support, you need to anticipate these anxiety-producing factors. Even if they don't come up explicitly, you have to suspect that they are there. Remember that the last rule of persuasion is "Be prepared to handle opposition."

It also helps to involve your supporters in the formation of the idea or proposal. If you take a completely finished idea to a peer and ask for an endorsement, you may run into resistance because of the "not invented here" syndrome. But if you take the ingredients to your peer, and ask for his or her help in putting them together, you may get more enthusiastic support. The other person has a chance to become one of the owners of the idea or project.

When you do encounter resistance, don't get defensive or angry. A certain amount of opposition to a new idea proposed by someone else is inevitable. Your cause is not lost if you treat the resistance as natural and not necessarily threatening. Follow these recommendations for dealing constructively with objections, hesitations, or opposition from a peer from whom you've asked support or help:

1. *Relax.* Sit back in your chair. Keep your facial expression attentive but free from frowns. When you look relaxed, you look confident, in control. You also make it easier for others to discuss your idea or proposal openly

in front of you, so you can learn what is behind their resistance.

2. *Listen.* It's not easy when you're feeling frustrated, defensive, or worried, but it's important because when you don't listen, you commit two sins. First, you don't learn what you need to know, and second, you risk offending the other person who feels that he or she has the right to express an opinion. Maintain frequent eye contact while you listen, so the other person knows you value what is being said.

3. *Accept.* You don't have to agree with the substance of the resistance. For example, if the other person is concerned that higher management will never buy your idea because it will involve too great an initial outlay of money, or if your potential ally says your idea won't work, because it was tried before unsuccessfully, don't dispute the objection. Accept the other person's feelings. Don't say anything that could translate as, "You're wrong," or "That's ridiculous." No one likes to have his or her feelings discounted or ridiculed. Thus, an important factor in influencing others is to accept their feelings.

4. *Move on.* After you've accepted the other person's feelings, discuss some other positive aspect of your idea. Here's how you might handle it: "Yes, I can see that the cost is a consideration in your mind, but here's something else you might want to think over. Under this system there would be less chance for error. We could probably reduce the rate of errors by half or even more." Giving another benefit may divert the opposition; it may not. If the objection of cost comes up again, you might want to accept it again, and give yet another benefit.

5. *Qualify the objection and answer it briefly.* If you believe that the cost problem is what is causing the resistance in your coworker's mind, deal with it. You might say, "Yes, I know this is going to cost more, but I think I can show how the initial outlay will be covered in less than twelve months. Would that take care of your problem?" If the answer is yes, go ahead with all the ammunition you have. Chances are you'll get at least a tentative commitment.

Most people show negative reactions to any resistance or difference of opinion. If you do, you risk losing control of the situation. Remember your superordinate goal, to get support for your idea, project, or proposal, and don't lose sight of it.

Remember also that when people voice objections or opposing opinions to your idea, they are responding. You've succeeded in getting them involved. There's nothing more disheartening than to sit down with a colleague, give your "presentation," and get no definite response one way or another. When you do experience this frustration in an interview with a colleague, you might say, "What are some of the pluses of this idea, as you see it?" Listen carefully. If the other person describes some benefits, then say, "What would have to happen for you to work with me on this?" You may uncover the final obstacle.

Of course, you'll probably get less resistance from some of your colleagues if your ideas have a record of getting acceptance and if they work. They'll want to be associated with a winner, and you'll have a better chance of keeping these people on your side if you give them as much publicity and credit as you can. For example,

"Sam here was the key to my pushing this. When I went to him with the idea, I wasn't sure how strong it was. But Sam saw its merit and encouraged me. He gets a lot of credit." Or, "Mary Jane was the one who put it together. I had pieces of an idea. She found the glue. So thanks to you, Mary Jane, for a workable idea." It costs you little to share your credit and glory. But the payoff can be tremendous. Sam and Mary Jane will want to work with you again. You're a winner in their eyes, and so are they.

Of course, as you become more successful, you will find some of your peers more reluctant to help you win. They are your competitors on the power track; it's best that you know who they are.

GATHERING INFORMATION

If you've ever found yourself surprised by a development that you should have known about but didn't, you know how helpless it feels. You didn't have the necessary information, and you know that having certain kinds of information gives you power. You can then take the initiative, or be on your guard, or anticipate someone else's move. You don't have to suffer unpleasant surprises or be left without options. Gathering information that will enhance your personal power should be high on your list of priorities. It should be accomplished systematically, not just by tapping the grapevine from time to time. Some recommendations:

Be more approachable. You're busy, true, but not too busy to take some time off to ask people, "What's new?" Leave your door open as much as you can to encourage callers. Be available. Don't convey the message through words or tone that you don't appreciate being interrupted or visited. Get out there and start calling on others for an occasional chat. If you get around, others will come to understand that you don't mind seeing them in your office.

Cultivate the right sources. Information gathering is a continuing and involved process. No one person is likely to tell you everything he or she knows. You get facts from one colleague, opinions from another, rumors from a third. These bits and pieces must all be put together in order to determine exactly what is going on. Thus, the more sources of information you have, the more knowledgeable you will be.

However, some sources will be more profitable than others. These are the ones to cultivate most actively, because they can generally be trusted to supply the kind of information you can use to advantage. For example, you may want to cultivate certain professionals and experts in the organization who can explain how their work may affect you. Other good sources are those who believe with you that information can be power. When you approach them, you give them an opportunity for power by doling out information to you. They win, and so do you.

Reciprocate. People won't feed you information forever without getting something in return. You're privy to information that would interest a lot of people, especially if your sources are plentiful and reliable. Make a point of passing on what you can, again, not always to the same people. Linking up with the grapevine means reaching out as well as taking in. The more you sow, the better you reap.

Be alert to significant areas. Not all types of information can be put to immediate use, but certain information can often trigger action that will later be beneficial to you. From a friend in marketing, you learn that a new position of senior vice president is being considered, that his boss is a candidate along with your boss. Even though it's all very hush-hush, you can start laying plans for moving up. First, you have to let your boss know you're interested, although you can't let him or her know about the news you've received. Second, you arrange your own succession, should your boss be selected.

Keep updating your connections. In order to be effective, your information network should reflect present concerns and issues, but some of your connections may have become obsolete. If they tie you down with irrelevant information, don't spend much time with them. Also, some people drift out of the mainstream. You may keep contact for old times' sake, but the value of their information is now suspect, because they are far removed from the action. Don't cut yourself off from any previous vein of information. Even if once in a while you still get a nugget, don't feel that you have to go to former lengths to maintain it.

Protect your sources. You should feel obliged to protect individuals who have passed on useful information that is not generally available. Don't make them suffer for having passed it along to you, otherwise you may never get gossip from them again. When you hear questions such as, "Where'd you hear that?" you might respond, "I'm trying to remember who mentioned it to me. I've had a number of things said to me lately." The other person may not fully believe you, but chances are the matter will drop, and if you persist in your lapse of memory, the other person will give up.

Get to know whom you can trust. Some people will be indiscreet, go too far, or talk too loosely. You'll get to know whom you can trust and whom you can't. Furthermore, you'll get to know who usually has accurate information and who doesn't.

Treat really scandalous information with great care. Who is sleeping with whom? Who is the target of charges of sexual harassment? Who got drunk and threatened to sock the CEO? Be awfully careful with this information. One promising young executive passed a hotel one night and saw the company's president with the woman who was personnel director. He told someone about it, who obviously told someone else about it. Unfortunately, his name was used in connection with the story: Who saw them? Al did. At the next meeting Al attended with the president, Al noticed that the president avoided speaking to him. At one point during the proceedings, Al happened to glance at the president, and saw the older man glaring at him. It was a juicy tidbit, but Al paid a dear price for it. People in the organization may pass your name along with the gossip out of mischief or malice.

Information is essential to you. It alerts you to forthcoming developments in the organization. It points to the emergence of new power figures and the decline of older ones. It is currency that helps you establish relationships with your peers. It gives you a key to the power dynamics of the organization, where the power is going, who has it, who has lost it.

If you are seen as a person in the know, you will soon have the respect and the attention of others, who want to be close to someone who is on top of things. Having the reputation of being a knowledgeable person increases your power. People will trade information with you, quote you, and consult you.

BUILDING COLLABORATION

You have a project in mind that involves another group. The result of your plan is a project team that involves personnel of both departments. The objective of the team is to develop the prototype of a new product that you've been imagining for months. You figure it would be an efficient, cost-effective way to allocate people, resources, and money to the development of this new product. You need the participation of the other department because there are technical experts there that you don't have.

The other manager agrees with your concept, and he offers to work with you on the proposal to higher management. You realize the benefits of having him collaborate with you. It would look better to higher management if two of you proposed the group. The other manager would automatically support you; you wouldn't have to worry about later resistance. In addition, the proposal itself would probably be stronger with his specialized perspective.

There are long-range benefits to you from such a

collaboration. If it works, you'd have a considerable ally ready and happy to join you in future ventures, and to provide support. It will also be good PR for you, both at the peer level and with higher management, *if it works*.

If you've ever committed yourself to a collaboration, you know how fraught with peril it can be. If it does not work, and it often doesn't, you'll probably lose a friend and an ally. You may even make an enemy or competitor. The benefits are there, true, but so are the pitfalls.

There are certain recommendations you should take seriously in trying to build a collaborative relationship with a coworker:

Expect that your methods will differ. How you work together, when, and what you hope to have come out of the working sessions, all have to be discussed. You should each explain how you prefer to work when you go it alone. For example, Person A tends to put things off until she feels extreme pressure, then devotes 100 percent of her time and energy to get the job done. Person B likes the plot each step of the way, finishing each part in an orderly fashion over time. Person C prefers passing notes and memos containing ideas and thoughts back and forth, while D usually chooses to sit down with colleagues and bounce ideas off one another even if it takes hours at a time. Person E finds details repugnant, while her partner, F, insists that every *i* be dotted before going on to the next step.

Negotiate your work methods. Ideally you come up with a way of working that both of you feel comfortable with, but it's more likely that you'll compare preferential methods and arrange to compromise. You will ask your partner to do some of the tasks your way, and you'll prepared to reciprocate.

Make your initial suggestions tentatively. Before you start the project is the time to discuss, to suggest, to negotiate. Put up trial balloons: "Here's how I thought we might begin. What do you think?"

You can hardly expect instant agreement. For one thing, you need time to develop mutual trust and respect. Each of you will have to try different ideas and methods and be prepared to back off when they don't work.

Go slowly at first. Take time in the beginning to work through the difficulties of the relationship. If you don't, later you may have to stop some critical phase of work in order to deal with problems that were ignored or suppressed at the outset.

Face problems immediately. Any suppressed feelings of tension and frustration will not only get in the way of the work, but will probably come rushing out in a destructive scene that can impair the relationship. You may want to refer back to the assertive-responsive mode of behavior. When you have a problem, describe it, tell your collaborator how you feel about it, ask the other person for his or her perception of the situation and feelings about it, then agree to work together to find a solution and a renewed commitment.

Give feedback. You assume that your collaborator realizes how much you value his or her work, but your collaborator may not. As you progress through each unit or stage, try to get across the message you want to give. If the other person's work is good, express your appreciation. If it isn't up to the quality you want, and if you think it can be improved, be tactful but forthright in your suggestions. Let your manner show that this is a partnership, not an "I'm-on-the-top, you're-on-the-bottom" situation. Solicit feedback on how you're doing.

Be prepared to do more. You initiate the project, and you may have to do more than your partner if you want the project finished your way. Even though you and your partner agreed on dividing up the work, you may be chagrined to discover that the other person hasn't done his or her share. Take up the slack. It's better than stewing and losing an ally over your anger. Put your feelings aside, and ask, "How about my giving you a hand?" or, "Want me to take over that section?"

Most people recognize that collaboration is extremely difficult, but in organizations, if you want to get things done through your peers, and if you want to form lasting and powerful working relationships with co-workers, you're going to have to enter into collaborative arrangements. If you transcend the difficulties, you'll soon be known as a person who can work with others to get things done.

FORMING ALLIANCES

There is power in numbers. A group of branch store managers discovered this. Coming together in a training class, they soon began to talk about their respective problems in running their stores and in communicating with the district office. Each manager complained that his requests for personnel or for equipment often went unanswered. There were other problems, such as the slow processing of personnel forms in the district office. Merit pay raises took an intolerably long time to be approved. At the end of the two-day session, one store manager said, "Why don't we continue this talking together?" They formed a small store managers' group to discuss problems, and trade answers and solutions. They defined common problems they were having with the district office and met as a body to take them up with the district manager. With his permission, the managers held monthly meetings over breakfast in a local restaurant. After a few months, some of the managers described their success to me: "We've gotten a lot of the complaints cleared up. Now our communications seem to be taken seriously. We have a lot of power we didn't have before."

It is typical of a bureaucracy that the people in power do not give it up until they have to. The district manager had seen no need to share his power, to pay much attention to the repeated complaints until they came from everyone at the same time. Suddenly the managers who had maintained all along that they had no power had quite a bit of it.

It's important to emphasize that this was no revolt of the barons against the king. The managers obtained permission to meet. In fact, their information organization was a direct outgrowth of the company-sponsored training program. They simply continued the activity. Furthermore, they were not hostile. They said, "We have problems that keep us from doing a good job. Here they are." They listened to the district manager as he told of his problems with them and their stores. Their alliance was friendly to the company; they were not organized to frustrate the achievement of the organization's goals, as some information organizations are. They formed themselves instead to increase the chances of achieving those goals. They operated by permission and in compliance with company policies and regulations, but when they spoke as one, they were powerful enough for the company to have to listen.

You may see a need for such an organization in your own company, of managers, of specialists, or of professional people. As a group, you can wield a lot of clout. Singly, as with the store managers, your voices may go unheard. That won't happen if you speak as a concerned group interested in the well-being of the organization as a whole. But lest you be suspected of being a counterproductive or subversive organization, you might want to take the following precautions:

Create a logical group with common problems. You can be managers of certain functions or on a particular level. You don't want people there with disparate responsibilities and interests. Management may never be entirely comfortable with the idea of your group, but they'll probably be especially anxious if there doesn't seem to be a focus of the group, except, in their minds, to make trouble for higher management.

Get permission to meet on company time. If you take time off from your respective responsibilities, let management know, even if you don't believe you have to get formal permission. Management tends to be uneasy if they don't know what you're up to, so keep everything open and aboveboard.

Present issues as joint. Don't make demands. With your new strength as a group, you will be listened to and taken more seriously. Always discuss issues as needing solutions because they inhibit you in the effectiveness of your work. Don't cross the line and start saying, in effect, "Give us this, or else." You will then be labeled an undesirable pressure group, working contrary to the welfare and interests of the organization.

Give management credit for the solutions they work out with you. The corrections and improvements may be largely because you took the initiative. They may even have been worked out by you, but give management credit for having recognized how important it was to listen and work with you. You want them to feel good and rewarded for what they have done, so they'll want to continue doing it.

KEEPING YOUR POWER BASE STRONG

Your search to find cohorts on whom you can rely for support will be continuing. One of the best ways to do this is to create obligations on which you may want to trade at some future time. Support a colleague openly in a meeting. Introduce people who want to meet each other or who would benefit from knowing each other. Write congratulatory notes after promotions. Send memos supporting others' causes. Circulate compliments about colleagues in the grapevine. Put in a good word to the right person—and let it be known that you have. Offer suggestions to a peer on how to conduct a campaign for an idea or project. Endorse a colleague's bid to head up a committee, project, or task force.

Don't commit yourself unnecessarily, however. The fewer commitments you have, the freer you are to operate. Listen sympathetically to someone who wants to enlist your support, but be wary about publicly committing yourself unless you honestly feel you have something to gain.

Keep higher management support. Get connected up the line and retain as many of those connections as you can. When you have top people among your backers, your peers know it. That's often enough to get people on your level to cooperate with you.

Be ready for a switch in allegiances. Bear in mind that most alliances are temporary. For practical reasons, and in their own interests, one or more of your allies may switch their allegiance to someone else. There is little you can do about this except hope that you get advance notice. Accept it as part of the game.

By the same token, you may want to make changes, to end one relationship in order to form another. While you want strong new allies, you certainly don't want strong new enemies, so if you have to change positions, let your former allies down gently by explaining what you're doing and why—before you do it, if possible.

Don't give up former allies just because you have moved higher in the hierarchy. Many a mobile manager has made this mistake. They can drum up support for you indirectly. At very least, they can talk up your cause, and they may even be able to influence their bosses to back you up. For political and status reasons, you may not wish to associate with your former colleagues too frequently or publicly, but don't snub them. Contact them, chat with them, be solicitous toward them. Let them know you're still someone they can call a working friend. They may see you as someone able to help them, if the occasion arises, and they'll be loyal to you.

Be seen with power people. In the minds of many, you will be judged, at least in part, by the people with whom you associate. Cultivate the power centers. You'll find that they like to be cultivated by others because it's an affirmation of their power status.

USING YOUR POWER

When you want action on a particular idea or proposal, it's time to gather support, to enlist your allies, to put on a campaign. How you use your political power is just as important as how you build and maintain it. You want a maximum return with minimum adverse consequences. Here are some suggestions you'll want to take seriously:

Be discreet in your maneuvering. In general, it is unwise to give your political moves the flash and visibility of a cavalry charge. You are more apt to get the results you want by moving quietly, negotiating behind the scenes, and making as little fuss as possible. Some people bellow and bluster, making themselves obvious targets for their opponents. They become too predictable, too easy to read. You don't want people to be able to anticipate every move you make. Also, people who make a lot of noise tend to be ignored after a while. Others say, "Oh, there he goes again." You'll also find that many of your colleagues are more comfortable working with and for you if you don't make public spectacles of yourself—or of them. Indirectness and subtlety are the wiser course.

Use a selling approach to enlist help. You may be an iron fist in a velvet glove, but in the long run you'll be more effective if your political pressure is used in an agreeable and constructive fashion. Even if you have IOUs and the power to do someone in if that person doesn't back you up, always present your pleas for cooperation in selling terms: "Here is my idea, and here's why I think you'll want to back me up." Don't ever resort to intimidation. You'll not only risk the person's support in this venture, but in the future as well. Be positive and definite about your position, the facts you are putting forth, and the goals you want to achieve. Don't manipulate, and don't leave out any important factors that may surprise or embarrass your allies when they surface later.

Make your requests in reasonable proportion to others' debts to you. If you can enlist people in a course of action they believe in, it's easier all around. Ideally they ought not to feel tremendous risk in giving you the support you want. It is politically unwise to ask an ally to make a major commitment by publicly taking sides on a controversial issue to pay you back for a relatively small favor. Maybe he or she does owe you one, but save it for a smaller issue.

How much pressure can you apply? If another person is deeply indebted to you, you may be in a position to say, "I'd like to ask you to join me even though you have some reservations." However, don't dismiss genuine fear. If your ally is concerned about the risk to him or her, don't brush it away. Accept those anxious feelings. If you can allay your colleague's fears, fine; if you can't, back off for a while. The harder you push, the more you may reinforce the fear. You won't win a committed ally by fast talking, the support needs to build from within.

Don't commit your allies without their approval. If you are going to quote them or use their names in connection with a move you are advocating, let them know in advance and keep them informed on the progress you are making. Furthermore, if there are occasions when you would like active cooperation, let people know exactly what you'd like: "Chris, when we talk to Elizabeth, I would like to take the first few minutes to state our position. But once I've finished, feel free to speak up whenever you'd like. In fact, I'd like your active back-up."

Avoid Pyrrhic victories. No matter how much strength you have, don't force issues to the point where people give in but feel destroyed or humiliated. A political shoot-out may end with a carpet of corpses, including those of your supporters. Power plays should be aimed at building rather than destroying. Each time you win, you increase your power in the eyes of others. Your moves should always be undertaken with consideration for your backers. You may have no right to enlist your allies in a players-risk-all, winner-takes-all game.

As you build your power, and occasionally flex your muscles, you will automatically attract certain co-workers who identify you as a power center and want to be associated with you, just as you tried to become close to the power centers you defined. Other peers will undoubtedly consider you to be an actual or potential competitor. Some will certainly dislike you, others may even fear you.

If your concern is to be well liked, you are probably poorly advised to get on the power track. Power attracts people, but it does not necessarily create warmth and affection. Therefore your priority should not be to be liked, but to be respected. Whether people like you or dislike you, they must respect you. They must know that though they disagree with you, with what you want to do, you will not lie, cheat, or betray them. If you become a jungle fighter, to use Michael Maccoby's term from *The Gamesman,* and believe that only the fittest survive, then you will find yourself in a deadly game indeed. If you are seen as a predator, as a threat that should be destroyed, you are inviting preemptive or retaliatory action. Eventually someone will get you—if not by fair means, then by foul.

12

BUILDING POWER IN A GROUP

If you are eager to acquire a reputation as someone who knows how to get things done when others flounder, work on your meetings skills. People in responsible positions in organizations probably spend from one-third to one-half of their working schedules in meetings. Most important decisions are made by groups, or at least undertaken by them. This is a great opportunity to be visible. You will be visible if you are effective in a group, if you know how to guide the group to the results you want. Furthermore, if you *are* effective, you'll find many people grateful to you because they have found so many meetings boring and a waste of time. This is often because the appointed or official leaders of meetings often don't lead them properly; they don't know how.

What's more, most of the people who complain that they spend so much time in boring or unproductive meeting are not trained in meetings skills or group dynamics. Consequently they flounder, get sidetracked, or stumble when faced with the slightest resistance from others. Riptides and crosscurrents are rife in meetings, even when the participants know one another. Even experienced managers sometimes find themselves at the mercy of forces operating in a group, instead of in control, making the meeting work for them.

If you can make a meeting work, that is, achieve a significant objective acceptable to the group, then you can expect respect. Moreover, if that objective is important to you or helps you advance, so much the better. If there are higher level managers in the meeting whom you can impress with your leadership and expertise in control, that is better still.

Thus, do not join the legions of people who groan at the thought of attending meetings, or who tell you that committees don't do anything. Meetings can be your proving ground. They can be the means for you to prove you are an exception: You are in that small minority of people who know how to get things done through groups.

FORMAL LEADERSHIP

If you are the person who calls and chairs meetings, there are simple steps you can take to show your superior leadership skills, for example:

Always have an agenda. Never call a meeting unless you have a good idea of what you want the group to accomplish. You don't need to have the answer, solution, or decision in mind before you issue invitations to sit down at the conference table, but you have to have an idea of the track the group is to follow. I'll never forget the time I visited a federal agency to attend a meeting to discuss a consulting proposal my partner and I had submitted. We were ushered into an executive's office and told to wait while the interested managers were summoned. Several people arrived and we sat down. The executive opened by explaining what we were there to discuss. The subject had nothing to do with us. My partner looked at the executive and said, "No." Taken aback, the executive thought for a minute, then suggested another reason for the meeting. Again, my partner pointed out that the subject mentioned had nothing to do with us. Exasperated and frustrated, the executive looked at his colleagues around the table and blurted, "Why *are* we holding this meeting?"

Pick your group for the purpose. If it's to be a problem-solving or decision-making session, keep the group small. There is growing evidence from psychological research that the most creative groups are small and odd numbered—five, seven, or nine people. Perhaps because a majority is possible, such groups seem to be more relaxed and efficient. Without fear of stalemate, people seem more likely to say what they think, even if there is disagreement. Five is the number of people some researchers in group dynamics believe makes for optimum efficiency, freedom of exchange, and cooperation.

In even-numbered groups of say four or six, there are more disagreements and fewer suggestions. Because of the possibility that the group will split evenly, participants tend to be aggressive in pushing their ideas in order to avoid a split and achieve a majority. The decision therefore may not always be the best, reflecting not a consensus but the wishes of the more aggressive members.

As the group gets larger, the chance for individual participation gets smaller. As a result, the individuals attending a large meeting feel frustration, especially if they have come wishing to participate actively. During the meeting they may think of good ideas and pertinent comments or develop strong opinions, but often they are not able to voice these right away. It's annoying to think of an insightful, relevant response and then have to wait several minutes before you can deliver it. People in large groups compensate by offering fewer opinions but more information. Thus, the large group can be used most effectively to collect and disseminate information. The leader must exercise more control and direction than is desirable or effective in a small group.

If you want to limit the membership of your group, you can always explain to those who thought they should be invited but weren't that it was necessary to limit its size to accomplish your desired objective.

Stay within your time limits. An essential part of staying in control of your group is observing time limits. Starting on time is a power move. People will sometimes test you by arriving a bit late and forcing you—they hope—to delay the start of the meeting. If you are seduced into this, you lose power and the latecomer gains it. You will find that if you firmly stick to the starting time, you will reward the on-timers and you force the latecomer to be there on time or risk missing something important. If your tardy colleague insists on arriving after the scheduled starting time on a habitual basis, be sure that you do not make a fuss. Just ignore the person when he or she walks into the room and tries to apologize. The more fuss you make the more rewarded the latecomer will feel in being tardy. The latecomer wants attention and probably wants to challenge you. Don't give him or her attention and don't show any sign that you feel challenged.

End when you say you will, too. A reasonable maximum time for a meeting is from sixty to ninety minutes. Few people maintain much concentration after ninety minutes. The value of a time limit is not only the greater effectiveness because of a higher level of attention and a lower level of fatigue, but also the self-policing the participants engage in when they know they have only a certain amount of time. Setting and keeping to a time limit increases your control over the meeting because the conferees help you.

INFORMAL LEADERSHIP

There are leadership roles that everyone in a group can play. If you are the formal or appointed leader of the group, you'll find them valuable to stay in control, to retain power. If you are one of several participants, you'll find these leadership roles useful in gaining control, if only for a time.

1. *State the problem.* The problem should be defined in terms that will be understood by everyone in the room. All the information necessary to make the decision or to arrive at a solution should be included—resources, limitations, constraints, etc. For example, you might say, "There is only about $10,000 in the budget to cover the cost of any solution we come up with." Or, "Remember that whatever we come up with has to be done with the people we have now. There's a freeze on hiring."

By stating the problem or suggesting the solution, you can take early control of a group and prevent it from floundering in search of a mission. In fact, insist that the goals of the meeting be clearly stated before the discussion starts. Otherwise you leave the door open for a vigorous partisan to take over with his or her solution before you have agreed on what the group is supposed to accomplish.

Be careful about defining the problem so tightly as to limit discussion. To illustrate, you are taking a price beating on the West Coast. You might define the problem this way: "How can we get our goods to the coast and remain competitive?" But that suggests a limited solution: You presently manufacture elsewhere. You might in fact find it feasible to manufacture also on the West Coast. So you are better off defining the issue in less constrained terms: "How can we be competitive in the West Coast markets?" Remember that the more options you have, the more likely that you will arrive at a better decision.

2. *Clarify the problem.* If you suspect that the discussion is off the track, you may be tempted to say so, but this is poor leadership and usually causes resentment. You're putting down the people who have just been talking. Yet if you want to maintain or take control, clarify the problem, or ask that the people talking clarify the relationship between what they have been saying and the problem as you repeat it. If you feel that the talk has strayed off because people have forgotten or failed to understand the problem, explain it.

It may well be that the problem has to be clarified because it has changed. For example, there is some evidence that you should not market on the West Coast where you are not competitive but should instead concentrate on other geographical areas. The problem is now slightly different: "Should we market on the West Coast? If so, how can we do so competitively?"

Restating and clarifying the problem is a good way to get a wandering discussion back on track without offending people or shutting them off. If they realize without your telling them that they have gone off course, there will be fewer hurt or angry feelings because of your intervention.

3. *Develop alternatives.* Groups often tend to select one solution early in their discussion and ride with it to the exclusion of other options. The chances of this phenomenon's occurring are even greater when you have strong partisanship. Therefore, if you detect premature closure by the group, say that you're not sure that the group has uncovered all the options that might be considered. Suggest that everyone in the room be polled as to whether they have anything they want to add. It's possible that they have felt steamrollered and have clammed up. This is a useful technique to apply when you oppose one or more participants but don't wish to be seen as doing so. You're taking a very reasonable course of action. The fact that you're preventing the others from keeping control is secondary—in the eyes of others.

If you believe that the group is in fact being steamrollered, if a partisan group is vocal to the point of suppressing a fruitful group discussion, suggest a "round robin." Someone will stand at a blackboard or a chart pad and record proposed solutions from everyone in the room. Go around the table and give all members a chance to contribute. Any criticism or evaluation is prohibited during the idea recording. The only questions permitted are those asking for clarification. People will feel less intimidated in offering their ideas if they know they are not going to get critical feedback right after they do it, and if their contributions are among many others.

What if you are tempted to do the steamrolling? Anticipate that there will be others in the group who will be unhappy if you try. They may resist it in the meeting, and they may not. Although they are quiet and seemingly submissive you should not believe that you have ridden over any opposition. That opposition may well surface later in the form of sabotage to your solution, and in future meetings, people will be on guard to prevent your repeating your strong partisan behavior. It's always a risk to encourage discussions, but the chance of getting commitment from the group is better if you can survive that discussion with your idea at least fairly intact. You don't have to suggest a round robin, but you are well advised to make sure everyone in the room has had a say.

4. *Keep the discussion on the track.* If you feel that the discussion is wandering, point it out, but don't make a pronouncement: "We're off the track." As I've already pointed out, you may get some flak. Make it a group issue: "I have the feeling that we have gotten off the track. Do others here share that feeling?" You may get instant—and relieved—support. On the other hand, you may find that you are a loner. In this case, graciously accede to the majority.

If several agree with you that the discussion has

floundered, then you have a chance to take control. Restate the problem and supply your own thinking. Guide the group where you want it to go.

5. *Summarize.* There are times in a meeting when the flow of ideas has become so plentiful that people lose sight of what's been said, or people have become polarized in their opposition. At such a point you can step in and say something such as, "It seems to me that this is a fair summary of what's been said here today." Then summarize what you've heard from the various participants. If you've kept notes, and are fairly accurate in your summing up, you may find yourself a hero. At the very minimum, you've provided breathing space. People will thank you for that. You may also be useful in positioning the various combatants whose agreements and disagreements have gotten lost in the heat. If you manage to highlight the real issue, the stage will be set for you to make your contributions and get the group going in a direction you favor.

6. *Describe the consequences of the group's choice.* If the deliberation seems to be going against the position you favor, you can attempt to slow things down by explaining what in your view will happen as a result of the decision toward which the group is leaning: how it relates to bigger or longer-range goals, its possible effects, direct and indirect, the potential liabilities, etc. It's possible that no one else in the room was thinking that far ahead, and you may create enough doubt or caution to shift the discussion. It's a much more acceptable method of getting people to rethink what they're doing than saying, "I think you're wrong."

7. *Test member commitment.* This is a valuable technique whether the discussion is going with you or against you. Stop the proceedings to find out how involved and responsible the participants feel about the proposed decision or solution. Now is the time to make it possible for a member to express reservations or hesitations that might create problems later. Make sure that each member is willing to assume responsibility and is available to implement the proposal if necessary.

If the tide seems to be running against you, take this opportunity to give potential supporters of your position a chance to express their hesitation of the conclusions toward which the discussion is heading. If things are going well for you, you seal the commitment of people around the table. You do not risk having covert opposition later.

TAKING CONTROL OF A RAMBLING MEETING

You're sitting in a meeting that doesn't seem to be going anywhere. People quibble over semantics, ramble interminably. The meeting clearly needs leadership, since people can't even seem to agree on the meeting's purpose. If you are the chairperson, you may not want to seem to be imposing your will, especially if you have a clear idea of what you want the group to do. If you're a member of the group, you don't want to give the impression that you're trying to take over. That could be resented by both the group and the leader you are displacing.

Resist the temptation to move in quickly to fill the vacuum. You may assume that nothing is happening because that's the way it looks. The group—especially if its members are not accustomed to working together—may be trying to find cohesion. The various members are getting to know one another, even if their talk is not substantive.

Relax and observe for a time. This initial period gives you a chance to discover any currents that may be developing that diverge from the direction you hope it will take. Identify your potential opposition at this early stage.

When you feel it is time to step in, get the group's tacit consent to do so. You can say something such as, "I wonder whether I could throw some ideas out to see what kinds of reactions you have." Getting the group's consent to your efforts to move it along encourages everyone to listen carefully. You may also get some instant help from those who have been praying silently that someone would do something. If people still aren't ready to move on the substantive issues, you'll get a signal—no consent—that this isn't the time for you to push.

If you do get consent, or at least encounter no opposition, introduce your ideas in a brief, general form. Don't give people the impression that you've already worked everything out, that you were simply waiting for the right moment to take over. You can always add details as others begin to respond to your contributions. To reinforce the appearance of not imposing your will, give the others a chance to discuss what you've offered.

For a time, confine your role to clarifying your ideas when others have questions about them.

If you are tempted to press hard at the outset, you may bring the issue to the point of possible rejection. You may also hand your quiet opposition all your ammunition, some of which may be used against you. Keep something in reserve to use later should a vacuum or misunderstanding of your position develop.

The person who early in the meeting tries to dominate the session by talking a great deal, pushing for early votes, pressing his or her own proposals, and showing impatience may not detect any serious antagonism at the time. In fact, if the meeting is meandering, other members who are bored or restless will often welcome the person who steps in to shape things up. But when the group members have developed more confidence in their individual abilities to work together, a backlash can develop against anyone they see as trying to dominate the group.

There's a big difference between providing guidance and pushing a group. People usually will not resent guidance; they will however resist domination.

MORE ON CONTROL

There are techniques that enable you to gain or regain control when you are a member of a group. If you practice these techniques, you will be seen by others as positive, skillful, supportive, and as a leader. You will also gain potential allies who can support you in future group situations.

Mediating. You are sitting in a meeting and the spotlight is on two people who are arguing. You'd like to stop the useless wrangling and get the group back on the issues, and you suspect that others in the meeting feel the same way. You decide to intervene by mediating. It's important to note that mediating is not peacekeeping, which is anything but a strong role. Mediating acknowledges that a conflict exists. It does not necessarily mean smoothing over that conflict. Quite the contrary, when you mediate, you actually define the conflict in sharper terms. Here's how you make entry: "Let me interrupt, because I'm getting the feeling that the issues are getting fuzzy, and we're spending a lot of time that I think could be better used if we understood more clearly how each of you sees the issues."

That's a good start. You don't charge them with straying from the issues. Rather you tell them it's getting harder to know how to differentiate their positions. You don't put them down, you offer to help.

You turn to A and say, "If I understand what you're saying, you believe . . ." Then you repeat what you think A's argument. Get A's agreement that your interpretation is correct. If he or she doesn't agree, then ask for a correction. Repeat the process with B.

You've stopped a bad and frustrating situation. Take advantage of the intermission in the wrangling and the good will you've undoubtedly generated among the other members of the group to advance your own ideas. If you've stated them already, say, "That means there are three approaches on the table. Mine differs from those of A and B in that . . ." If you haven't already described how you feel, say, "Now that we have a firm fix on what A and B believe, I'd like to show how my suggestion differs (or fits in)." Your mediation has given you a chance to have the last (or at least the latest) word.

Harmonizing. Harmonizing is a less direct approach than mediating. As you sit listening to the disputants, you realize that they really are not far apart. They have simply ceased to listen to each other. You stop the arguments and summarize each position as you hear it, emphasizing the areas of near agreement. You thereby provide the group with some common ground to form the base of a constructive discussion. Harmonizing is especially valuable when tempers are running high or when the adversaries have become polarized.

Take the technique one step further by underlining any of their views that are close to yours. Even if they differ from your opinion, you can now invite others to discuss the respective merits of their positions and yours. You have in one stroke broken a log jam and provided another opportunity for discussion of your ideas.

Supporting. If the group does not seem receptive to new ideas, including yours, or if someone is dominating the group and keeping it under tight control, watch for the opportunity to give a colleague support. The minute he or she has thrown an idea out for consideration, you say, "That's an interesting idea. I wonder what others think." Or, "We should talk about that." If you don't agree with the idea, say, "I don't think I agree, but I think the group should discuss this." You might not be able to open the group up with your own contribution, but if you act in the group's best interests by suggesting strongly that someone else's idea be discussed, you can open the door to consideration of yours.

In general, one of the best ways to get support for your ideas is to support others' right to be heard. If you are seen as acting in the group's interests, concerned that the group achieve its objective, you'll have an easier time getting heard. If you are perceived as a dominator, you'll find resentment building. Eventually you'll be thwarted in your desires to influence the group.

You must also be on guard against certain obstructive behaviors. If you don't know how to deal with them, you can quickly become a victim who is silenced or sidetracked.

Shutting off. You're making a point. Someone interrupts you to say, "I really don't think that's on the subject," or the other person begins to talk about something quite different. If you sit there in silence, you will have lost control. You can say to the interrupter, "I would like to finish what I was saying," and then resume talking. If the interrupter charged that you have strayed from the subject, your response can be, "I think what I'm saying has much relevance and here's why," and then explain the tie. You can go an important step further and get group support: "That's why I think I'm very much on the subject. Do you others agree? If not, I'll drop my point. I'll stop talking." If one or more of the others agree that you were on target with your comments, the shut-off artist has been effectively handled.

Humor can be a way to shut someone off. For example, you become impassioned in making your point. A colleague breaks in with a smile to say, "Get Ted a soap box. He's really warming up." There will probably be some laughter. At this point you are extremely vulnerable. The humor was most likely an attempt to quiet you. As soon as the laughter has subsided, respond. You might say, "Stick around for the rest of the speech. I'm about to make my most important point." Then without getting more impassioned, present an aspect of your idea that you believe will grab the attention of the others. Benefit from the attempt to shut you off: You received feedback indicating that you were warming up too much. It was time to lower the emotional temperature and present your ideas in a more rational manner.

Sometimes the humor can be so personal as to border on being malicious. In the middle of your presentation of your idea, someone else mutters, "The last time we ran with an idea like that, we almost had to consider Chapter Eleven." There is some embarrassed laughter. The other person has tried to shut you off by labeling your idea extravagantly foolish. Your reaction: Don't join in the laughter. You'll be undercutting yourself if you do. Say something such as, "I'm sorry, I was interrupted. May I finish?" You'll usually find that you have the floor again. I've heard people respond this way: "I'm sorry. I didn't get the point. I think it was supposed to be humorous, but I didn't get the punch line." Sometimes this kind of response gets an embarrassed silence. On the other hand, your interrupter might feel he or she has the floor to expand on the point.

It's best not to yield the floor. When you are interrupted, quickly point it out to the group and ask that you have a chance to finish.

Making judgments. One of the other conferees suggests that you are angry, or defensive, or projecting as you talk or answer the opposition. The other person is trying to sidetrack you by getting you to try to defend yourself. Realize again that you are vulnerable, and don't let yourself be thrown off. Just say, "Well, I don't want to take up the group's time to discuss whether I am or not. I just want to make this point, which I think is very important." Make your point. Usually your refusal to debate the label the other person has put on you is sufficient to silence him or her.

Missing the target. You disagree with another's point and attempt at rebuttal. In the middle of your argument, the other says, "You've missed my point." A lot of time can be wasted arguing whether or not you missed the target. So, repeat what you heard the other say, get agreement or clarification, then resume your response. You'll make more impact on the group if you choose this course rather than to try to defend yourself.

MAKING IT A GROUP ISSUE

An important factor in being effective in a group is to remember that you are not an individual in a room with others but a member of a group. You can operate alone, or you can get a lot of support from the group, but to do this, others in the meeting must see that you are one of them and devoted to advancing the welfare of the group, that you are helping the group to achieve its objectives. Here are some ways you can emphasize your group membership:

Talk to the group. When you talk, it's natural to notice someone around the table who seems sympathetic to you and your ideas. You are probably getting a nod or two of agreement, giving you reinforcement. But, if you talk predominantly to this person, you risk making others feel excluded, and you will alienate them. Talk to everyone in the group. Learn to establish eye contact with everyone, even with those you know will oppose you. *Involve* your prospects.

Don't rush to defend yourself or to answer resistance. Someone rebuts your point, or asks you a question that implies some criticism of your viewpoint. Most people would rush to respond, but that can be a mistake. Remember, you don't want to stand alone if you can help it, and you don't want to appear defensive. So relax, look thoughtful, and let the other person know with a nod and an attentive expression that you are listening. Don't rush to say anything. Sometimes your silence will lead the other person to amplify his or her statement of rebuttal, which can give you ammunition with which to fire back when you're ready. Sometimes while you're sitting there, thoughtful, some other member of the group will respond for you. That person's statements will carry much more weight, since he or she is not speaking defensively. Don't interrupt someone who is challenging you, even though you're sure the other person is missing the point. Although wrong, your critic could be telling you something you need to hear, such as that you haven't been as clear as you need to be.

Look at your critic. Make a point of showing that you are listening carefully. You may be getting important feedback that tells you where you have not been effective.

Look for areas of agreement. Many members of the group will be negative and will nitpick. If you, on the other hand, are positive, showing the others where there is agreement on even minor matters, the group will have a sense of progress with the job. You can then move to resolving larger issues.

Get help. If you feel hemmed in by challenges and objections, you might say, "I guess I haven't made this clear," or "I haven't done justice to this. Can someone else help me?" You place the blame on yourself for a less than adequate presentation, not on their failure to understand or agree. You may indeed get help to close the gaps or satisfying reservations.

Be ready to compromise on minor points. Sometimes your willingness to give in on minor points will help you get acceptance of your major proposition, so know what you can concede.

Ask for action. A group sometimes needs to be nudged. Asking for action is also a good way to smoke out any hidden objections or reservations that otherwise may not have surfaced until later, or may never have been raised.

An essential part of leadership in a group is knowing when to take initiative and when to sit back and let the group do it. For example, if you need help or a breathing space because of opposition, you can always turn to the group and ask for help: "I'd like to know how some of you others feel about the idea I presented," or, "Well (you say to an outspoken critic), I think the group has heard plenty from you and me. Perhaps now we ought to hear from the others." You want the other members of the group to take some responsibility for what is going on.

Your silence may sometimes encourage this responsibility. I recall vividly when I was attacked by another member of a board of directors for a proposal I had submitted the meeting before, when my colleague had not been present, and which the board had passed unanimously. Although my colleague addressed the board and not me, everyone, I'm sure, recognized that she was saying that my proposal had been inappropriate. I felt defensive, and I wanted to respond to her attack, but I didn't. I just sat, looking at her attentively. After she stopped talking for a minute, another member of the board spoke up about the preceding board session, reminding my colleague that the board had deliberated the facts. Another member supported that statement, and then another. Very quickly, the dissident was isolated, reminded that she was questioning the unanimous judgment of the board, and was effectively silenced. I never had to say a word. And their response was so much more forceful than anything I might have said. It had become their issue. She hadn't anticipated that.

Sometimes you encounter a person who wants to take over the meeting. It usually is not in your interest to sit back and let the person become your competitor in influencing the group. Once again, you are well advised to make the domination a group issue:

Don't take on the dominator one-to-one. A battle between the two of you, with everyone else as spectators, still adds up to a performance, not a group discussion.

Don't leap into a negative role in countering the dominator's ideas. This will make you look obstructive, and if you fall silent, letting the dominator have the floor, you will look acquiescent.

Direct your remarks to the group as a whole. In

most meetings people talk to the originator of an idea, but if you get the other people involved, the chance for all-around participation is heightened. When the dominator advances a proposal, therefore, respond by looking around the table and talking to everyone.

Ask questions of other participants. When you talk to the others, invite comments. If the dominator interrupts, say, "I'd like to hear what Gloria thinks."

Head off premature votes. A common tactic of the dominator is to push for a vote when he or she thinks everything is going the "right" way. When that happens, say, "I'm not sure we are ready to close this out. I'll bet there are some more points to be made." If you get support, you'll have eroded the strength and influence of the takeover artist. If you don't, you'll probably still be seen by the group as an expediter.

ARRIVING AT A CONSENSUS

If you lead a group and want not only the best decision or solution, but also hope for the greatest commitment from the participants to that decision or solution, try for a consensus. A consensus means that everyone believes that, given all the considerations and constraints, they've found the best product of the group deliberations. People don't just go along, or vote with the majority. They really invest themselves in the decision. It takes a special leadership skill to nurture a group along the rough road to a consensus. Some recommendations:

Give the group time. Decisions that are based on consensus generally involve much discussion, since it is expected that everyone involved will have a full say. The decision will come more slowly than with majority rule.

Encourage all participants to have a full say. Create an atmosphere in which people feel free to voice even their slightest concerns or reservations. They won't do that if they are cut off by others or made to feel that their concerns aren't worth consideration. Make sure no one gets put down or shut out. In the first stages of the discussion, you may want to discourage debate so everyone can express his or her opinion. Accept the fact that people are genuinely worried about what they say, and respect contributions even though you don't agree with them or believe they are very important. People will soon feel free to express what is on their minds if they know they will not be belittled or besieged.

Emphasize advantages. Participants will often discuss what they don't like about a proposal. That's necessary, but from time to time sum up what people around the table feel is good about it: "Granted, this will cost more money than the present procedure during the first three months, but after that it should reduce normal expenses by at least 10 percent."

Gauge the seriousness of reservations. Sometimes people value the chance to express even those reservations they don't take very seriously. See how serious their negative feelings are, and how much support they get in the group. Often when they find that others don't share their fears, they let go of them. Also, once people in the group tend to think more in a positive vein, they come up with suggestions for how their own objections can be overcome.

Keep summing up areas of agreement. With sufficient discussion and a clear respect within the group for everyone's contributions, you can expect areas of agreement to widen considerably. Eventually you will reach a point where problems or disagreements almost melt away. This comes at a stage when people begin to realize that they are approaching a decision that will be acceptable to all, that the group is working together to remove all remaining obstacles. Consensus may then emerge quite suddenly.

You may find that seeking consensus is hard for you. It is difficult for most, but especially so when you are conditioned to seeking power. This conditioning may lead you to push for a fast majority, which suits the power image better. The problem with a fast majority is that the decision may not remain firm. On second thought people may weaken in their resolve or commitment. With a consensus, however, you have a contract that most people feel obliged to honor, and the more firm the contract you have with people, the more power you enjoy.

NEUTRALIZING THE "NO" PEOPLE

In any group situation, one of the most formidable obstacles to your power and control is the nay-sayer. Groups are often quite well-disposed to the person who, at critical moments of deliberation, says such things as, "I don't think we can get approval for this," "We tried that a couple of years ago, and it didn't work," "It's not in the budget," or "Why don't we table this (or form a committee) and take time to think about it more." The reason the nay-sayer has such power in a group situation is that it's easier and less risky for a group to turn down or postpone consideration of a proposal. You usually have to take certain steps to overcome the impact of the person who is eager to be negative. For example:

Clarify the risk. People hesitate to make a risky decision because no one wants to make a mistake. But, in some situations mistakes are less deadly than in others. In some cases, if a decision indeed proves to be a mistake, it will hardly bankrupt a company, but, on the other hand, if a decision is not made, there will be searching questions from up the line about why no action was taken.

If a negative response reflects fear of risk, put the decision in perspective. Show that the stakes are not as high as people think, or that the consequences of not making a positive decision could be worse for all concerned than those of taking a step that could fall short of success.

Sell the benefits harder. If you do not want to get into a debate, it may be time to resell the benefits in case some of the group members didn't recognize them fully the first time around. "Okay," you might point out, "this may fail, and some people will be unhappy that we decided to risk it, but we'll get some data that we couldn't get any other way." You may in fact be able to offer even more substantial reasons for a "yes" decision. Just try not to get defensive and argumentative. Stick to selling the benefits.

Multiply the leadership. Sometimes when pushing for a project, you can anticipate opposition not just because of disagreement with your thinking but also because of objections to your leadership role in presenting the idea. If you sense a confrontation on that issue, you might say, "I guess everyone can see how Mark feels, and you know where I stand. I'd like to hear from the people who haven't said much." You may find others in the group who can be encouraged to lend support to your position.

Confront the negative behavior. The person who keeps throwing up opposition may not be aware of the negative role he or she is playing. After you've resold the benefits, you may want to ask some straightforward questions: "Why the pressure to hold off?" "How do the dangers outweigh the possible benefits?" "What's the worst that can happen if we go ahead with this?" Or confront the nay-sayer: "Look, I think you are closing out chances to consider this fairly."

MAKING A PRESENCE
IN A PRESENTATION

More and more managers are enrolling in public-speaking seminars, courses, and workshops. The reason, of course, is that visibility in an organization is precious, and you are seldom more visible than when you are addressing a group of co-workers. Relatively few do it well. Those who do are remembered, and often asked to give other presentations. The more visibility you can achieve, the more attention you may get from the power centers. You are indirectly bidding for more responsibility and authority, more prestige, and more power.

To be successful in making presentations, you must exercise control over your material and yourself. You should project an image of self-confidence, and appear in command of the situation. This is a prime opportunity for you to create a presence, to project your personal power.

Not everyone, of course, is a compelling public speaker. You may be well advised to take a course or a workshop in which you can practice before a live audience and get valuable feedback. It could be one of the best investments of time and money you'll ever make. In the meantime, the following recommendations are ones that almost anyone can put to work advantageously:

Take the center of the table or the room. It's a leadership position. You may be tempted to be informal and talk from your seat, but if you do, you give up something valuable—center stage.

Start slowly. It may take people a short time to get in a listening mood. Don't hit the ground running, they may miss some of your opening remarks. Also, if you are even the least bit nervous, starting slowly will help you calm down. If you begin too fast, you'll risk stammering and stumbling. Gradually increase your rate of speaking as you feel more comfortable.

Look around the room. This is one of the hardest rules for speakers to remember. You are addressing everyone in the room, so establish eye contact as frequently as you can. Every few sentences, sweep the room with your eyes. There's always the danger of your locking in on someone who seems attentive and sympathetic, but if you do that, you make others feel left out. Their minds will wander.

Stand tall. Be an imposing presence, even if you're short. Don't slump.

Don't bury your nose in your notes. You will lose the interest of your audience if your nose is pointed downward. If you must consult your notes, do so quickly then raise your head before you resume speaking. Otherwise your voice will be constricted and sound less impressive.

Speak up. Make sure at the outset that everyone in the room can hear you. There's nothing more distracting than to have people remind you to speak up so they can hear.

Don't fidget. Don't jingle coins in your pocket or play with a pencil. People will start watching your hands rather than listening to your words.

Let people know how you will answer questions. If you are giving information to them for the first time, give it as a piece, then take questions. This is usually preferable to interrupting your presentation for them. Others will get impatient because they are not hearing what they want, and your flow will be interrupted. Remember that most people have short spans of concentration. A solid presentation of twenty to thirty minutes is fine, followed by a questions-and-answers period. People can't sit still for much longer than that. Letting people interrupt you to ask questions is all right when you are dealing with familiar information. If you have large amounts of data to transmit to your audience, break up your presentation with Q-and-A periods. You may refer to some of your information in your presentation, when you don't want to be exhaustive, and invite questions at the end if people want to know more about it. This will keep your presentation flowing.

Keep answers short. You may want to impress your audience with your command of the subject, but when you take a long time to answer one person's question, you may be boring others. So keep your answers concise. If someone wants to know more, he or she can ask a follow-up question. If the questioner threatens to dominate the period, suggest that you take some other questions and come back later.

Face your audience. Visual aids can be a help your presentation, but don't talk to them. Refer to them if you must but try to face the group when you talk.

There are other recommendations that you should consider. Try to get your key point up front. Let your group know immediately why they should sit there and listen to you. Some presenters are coy, they like to build suspense. It usually annoys the audience. So answer the question, "Why should these people listen to me?" Present a benefit to them early on, and when you're finished, tell them what you want them to do. Ask for action: an agreement, commitment, decision, etc. If you don't make it clear what you want, you may not get anything.

If you are asked to make an impromptu presentation before a group, take a minute and use the acronym KEY to shape your talk. The letter K stands for your key point. What is the principal fact or benefit you want to present? E is short for explanation and expansion. Give the necessary supporting information to back up the fact or justify the benefit. Finally, Y is the windup (remember the windup keys for toys). Summarize what you've said quickly and give people a sense that they have heard an integrated, complete (though short) presentation.

It takes a great deal of practice and sensitivity to become skillful in informal as well as formal group leadership. But as you become more competent in your meetings, you will stand out. First, you will become prominent because so many others lack your talents in running or participating in meetings. Second, you will stand out because you know how to help the group achieve its objectives. You'll be the person that people turn to in a meeting when there is floundering, frustration, conflict, or deadlock.

HEADING A COMMITTEE OR TASK FORCE

People make fun of committees, and the government has given task forces a bad name. Nevertheless, leadership of an important committee or task force can provide you not only with visibility and increased prestige, but it can also lead to greater power and responsibility. A few years ago, an acquaintance of mine was one of many young editors in a magazine publishing company. One of the company's trade publications was suffering from declining subscriptions. It was generally considered dull, the editorial direction, uninspired. The company had the wisdom to gather a task force of experienced editorial personnel to determine what could be done with the ailing publication. My young acquaintance had the wisdom to persuade management to let him have a place on the task force. He served well, exhibiting such enthusiasm and contributing so substantially that when the task force had revamped the sick magazine, he was named to replace the former managing editor who was forced to resign. He was the youngest managing editor in the company, and he succeeded in making what had been a liability into a very profitable asset.

Task forces are especially advantageous to an ambitious, power-building person, because task forces, by their very definition, are interdisciplinary, multifunctional, semiautonomous, temporary problem-solving or decision-making groups that often win responsibility for executing what they devise. For example, in a large paper company that was planning to build a new processing plant in the South, a task force was formed to make sure that the plant was state-of-the-art and that its human resources would be well-prepared through training and development, as well as proper hiring. So professionally impressive was the task force's work, that many in the group became the nucleus of the plant's management.

You may find opportunities to suggest the formation of a temporary problem-solving group. The best place to look for reasons to form such a group is in the systemic or interdepartmental area. The problems that exist in the system or between functions of the system are promising material for a task force. They are often problems that cannot or will not be solved by the managers responsible for the functions, because they are too close to the problems or individually they don't have the authority to tackle them. A task force formed to deal with those problems must have a higher umbrella of authority. If you are designated leader or even a member of such a group, you probably are operating with higher authority than you normally would. Be careful about taking on such a group that is formed by the managers involved. You'll become a negotiator in what is probably a no-win situation for you. If possible, establish as a condition for your leadership that the authority for the task force emanate from a management level higher than they are. That way, if there is a deadlock or polarization, you have a higher authority to appeal to, and someone who can save your neck.

If you are given responsibility for the recruitment of members of your task force, choose the most experienced, competent people you can get. It won't be easy to persuade their managers to release them, but if the departments will be affected by the solution, you can argue that they will want to have input and some influence over the results of the group's work. You can also subtly point out that they may want to be represented by the best person possible, not just by someone they can easily spare. Their prestige is also at stake.

Once you have your task force going, you want it to be a success. Its success will no doubt be yours. You will have proved that you have much problem-solving ability, creativity, and leadership skill. A successful task force is a springboard. Take the following suggestions very seriously:

Treat all members as equals. There will probably be two or three members of the group with whom you can work exceptionally well, but try to build good working relationships with the others, although you may not know them so well or be so comfortable with them.

You don't want them to feel like outsiders, because they may sabotage the work of your group (and you in the process). Also, don't discuss task force business with some members of the group outside the group. The others will resent the behind-the-scenes activity.

Share your contacts with higher management. One of the perquisites of being a group leader is that you have the channel to higher management. It is your job to maintain such a liaison, but not monopolize it. Reporting all the group's actions or deliberations to management, and then relaying all the upper-level reactions or decisions back to the group, is certain to generate the suspicion among your colleagues that they have been excluded from the real action. To counteract feelings of being left out, occasionally invite the higher-level people with whom you consult to meet with the group.

Let everyone share the glory. If your group is very successful, you can afford to let others share the credit. If you draft a report, put everyone's name on it. If you give a verbal presentation, mention the names of your confreres. You may orchestrate, but let some of them share the presentation with you.

Give members an identifiable piece of the action. Have members of the task force assume responsibility for specific segments or phases of the project. When people own part of the action, they commit themselves more. You'll build cohesiveness in the group, and you'll get a lot of credit outside, because each member of the group will be talking to his or her boss, and the boss is more likely to join in if a subordinate is responsible for the work.

When the group has finished its work, report the results in written form, even if you are told that a verbal report is sufficient. Summarize and describe the work of the group—its methods and results. Distribute the report, complete with credit for everyone, to the managers of the people involved, the sponsor of the task force and whoever provided its umbrella or authority, and higher management, if you get the permission of your sponsor. If the results are impressive, your sponsor should have no problem giving you permission to publicize your achievements and his or her good judgment in giving you the assignment.

13

BUILDING YOUR
POWER FROM OUTSIDE

You may well find bricks outside your organization with which to build your power base within. You can earn a professional reputation in a number of ways. You can write books or articles, lecture at colleges and universities as part of their professional or management development curricula, give seminars and workshops, hold office in associations or community volunteer groups, or become recognized as a speaker for all kinds of meetings, conferences or conventions. However, going outside to enhance yourself inside has some potential pitfalls that you should consider:

Make sure that your outside activities are relevant to the organization. Appearances at the local Kiwanis Carnival as a magician are not usually conducive to power building. Whatever you do on the outside must relate to something you do or would like to do on the inside. For example, if you are marketing director and write or lecture on how to develop strategic planning, you can probably benefit from your extracurricular activities. The functions are closely related, inside and out.

Get your company's permission to conduct your outside activities. In some enlightened organizations, you will be seen as an external PR person. They'll subsidize you because they see what you do as a reasonable cost for making themselves look good. In other organizations, when you try to be active away from your office, you can expect to encounter much grumbling, some jealousy, and even anger over the money you are costing the organization by not being at your desk all the time like everyone else. These organizations resent having to support your "hobby." If you are going to be successful at outside professional activities, you need support and approval from within. If you try to operate without it, you will risk not only your power, but your job.

Develop a career plan for yourself. Have a rationale for doing what you do outside. Learn to deal with extracurricular currency, otherwise you won't get the power you want, only a certain prestige, applause, and envy. The personnel director who takes to the road to publicize his company's advanced cafeteria benefits plan may come back to the office where he started and stay there, or he may get so busy in the Personnel Managers' Association, holding offices and winning awards, that he loses sight of his power track in the company. Know, therefore, what you really want to do with the prestige and honors you accumulate outside. What are they expected to buy for you on the inside?

Of course, you may undertake outside activities to get a better position elsewhere. That's fine. It's a great way to build a reputation and a network. Interestingly, you may find that as you become better known to search firms and other companies, you become more sought after and valued by your present organization. That's using leverage legitimately.

Books. Writing a book on a business, managerial, professional, or technical subject can provide you with an exceptionally fine opportunity to promote yourself. Be warned that you won't make much money from the venture, but that presumably isn't your primary reason for authoring the book. You're after the prestige it can gain for you. Some people will be impressed, knowing what a difficult project it is; other people won't be if they don't know how much work goes into a book.

Understand that you will have to do much of the promoting. The publicity department at your publisher can be helpful in arranging some local television and radio coverage as well as an interview in your area newspaper. Chances are your community's service clubs, P.T.A., and such are on the lookout for speakers, and you can let them know that you are available. Your publisher will also send review copies to your industry or trade press if you supply a list of publications. Some of them will review the book, and you may hear from an editor who would like to do an interview or an article about you.

That's about as far as the publisher goes. There probably won't be much advertising, so for the most part you're on your own. Invest in a number of copies at your author's discount (about 40 percent off list). Make sure the powerful people in your organization have copies, preferably with individual messages on the flyleaf. Some of these people will happily display your book on their bookshelves. See that your company library has a copy, and notify the editor of your organization's newsletter or magazine.

Send books to influential people outside your organization, in your trade, industry, or profession whom you wish to impress. Your publisher will send books for you, but they will probably arrive with impersonal cards saying, "With the compliments of the author." You'll make a bigger splash if you send them out yourself with handwritten or typed notes that personalize the message. The more recognition you receive from outside your organization, the greater will be your credibility inside.

If you're planning your first book, here are some words of advice. Don't write a manuscript without finding a publisher. You can find a listing of book publishers in the current volume of the *Literary Market Place* in your local library. Send short query letters to a selected group of publishers describing in a paragraph or two what kind of a book you plan to write, and for what audience. Enclose a short biography of yourself. If an editor responds favorably, he or she will most likely ask you for an outline of the book and one or two sample chapters (to demonstrate that you can write). The next step is a contract, after which you write the book. In some cases, you may get a small advance.

One final note, if you plan to write about anything involving your organization, get top-level clearance in writing before publication.

Articles. In some cases you may get even more mileage out of an article in a trade, business, or professional publication than you get from publishing a book.

You'll get your name before some very influential people. Some magazines will supply you with reprints or authorize you to reproduce your own. Just as with the books, you can send copies with personal messages to lots of people. You'll probably have a larger readership than with a book, as people tend to read more magazines.

Use the query approach with magazine editors also. A positive response from an editor increases the chance of commitment to publishing your article.

Professional or volunteer associations. There's much prestige and publicity in getting involved with volunteer groups, whether they are community, charitable, industry, or professional. I have my own experience as testimony. A few years ago, I became active in the New York City chapter of a large professional association. I eventually became president. I won't pretend that I did it for altruistic reasons, I don't know who does, I was making a transition in my career from an organization to private practice, and I wanted the exposure.

Much of the exposure came with the office, which, I discovered, enjoyed tremendous prestige. Despite my credentials—a successful career, lengthy involvement in the field, dozens of articles and several books—I never possessed more credibility and importance than I did as president of the chapter. I was consulted, quoted, even asked to promote books and products. I had immediate access to high level executives and professionals. I received widespread respect and recognition.

Some of the exposure, however, I orchestrated. For example, the chapter had a fine newsletter. Each month I wrote a "president's message," which had never been done on a regular basis by my predecessors. I also saw to it that my picture accompanied each monthly message. Soon I was known by about 2000 people, many of them very influential in the field, many of them in the largest, best-known corporations in the country.

You can achieve comparable publicity for yourself in an association. On the local level, you can get involved with a charitable drive or a volunteer group. Your picture will be in the newspaper. You will be asked to appear on TV or on the radio. You will be invited to speak before clubs. All of your activities are suitable material for the house organ.

Seminars, courses, workshops, and lectures. Many organizations offer public seminars and workshops. No doubt many of their brochures cross your desk weekly. Some of them hire people on a part-time basis to run those workshops. You might send some letters to the sponsoring organizations describing your areas of specialization, what kinds of sessions you would like to design and conduct, and your background.

Your industry or professional association may be fertile ground for you. If they have local, regional, or national meetings, they probably have need for workshop presentations and lectures. Get your name out there.

A nearby college or university may be interested in you as an adjunct professor to teach a course or two from semester to semester. Teaching can be a source of much prestige and distinction.

In all of these activities outside your organization, you have to know that your company supports you. Otherwise there will be grumbling and gossip about your loyalties and energies being invested elsewhere. Another issue is whether you are free to accept fees when you work elsewhere on company time. Some organizations, as I've pointed out, are happy to see you be successful in the larger arena—as long as you don't neglect your responsibilities "at home." Others say that if you charge for your services, then you should either forfeit your fees to the company or take a vacation day. It's always best to have a policy statement on this in advance, and in writing.

Your celebrity will likely build your colleagues' respect for you, although the respect may sometimes be grudging. Your success will be confirmed when colleagues, high managers, and professionals begin to consult with you in the areas you have achieved distinction. Eventually you may be invited to sit in on planning, policy, or development meetings in which your contribution will stamp you as someone valuable.

14

POWER, CULTURE, AND CONFLICT

Every organization has its own culture, reflected in its objectives and concerns, the managing style of its managers, its traditions and heroes, its relationships with employees, clients, and shareholders, even in the informal as well as formal, dress codes. The organization's culture relates to its values, priorities, and even structure.

Generally, the most successful members of the culture are those who share its values, style, and outlook. Those members may not be the most successful in terms of financial practice, productivity, planning for the future, but judged by the criteria developed by the organization, they will be favored. Generally, too, the least successful, and often temporary, members of the culture are those who do not share its values and do not conform to the prevailing style. They insist on applying their own philosophies, techniques, and methodology that are at variance with "the way we do things here."

A maverick manager is often rendered less effective when coworkers move to isolate him or her. The maverick is cut off from communications, finds building collaborative relationships difficult, and is hampered in forming a power base of allies. In extreme cases the manager who is alien to the organization's culture is pushed into a backwater. Employees, sensing the relative powerlessness of their manager, will experience a lack of motivation. Ironically, an adept manager can come into a culture in which lack of motivation is rife, shape an effective work productive group, and still, if he or she is not sensitive to the demands of the culture, experience isolation as well.

Mavericks can survive in an alien culture, however, if your values are the same as those of the organization, and the way work fits in with the accepted modes of doing things, your job is much easier, and your chances of building power much greater. But even if you are essentially an "outsider," you can through competence, sensitivity, and discretion build constructive working relationships with your peers and bosses.

One of the outstanding examples of survival in an alien culture was furnished by a tax specialist with a major corporation. He came to work with no suit jacket or tie. He wore loafers. He bent the rules as far as he could without breaking them. He evidenced distaste for management. Yet no one moved against him, because he followed the recommendations outlined in the previous chapter. He became a widely recognized authority, frequently quoted and interviewed in the business press. He wrote countless articles and several books. There was a lot of grumbling, but he seemed quite invulnerable.

If your approach to management and motivation of people is substantially different from that encouraged and sanctioned by the organization's culture, you will probably need some protection. The best person to do that is your boss, but if your boss is more in tune with the culture than you are, you may be seen as a problem. If your employees hold you in high regard, work hard for you, perhaps harder than most employees in the organization, your boss may be suspicious of you, or if you are, say, very democratic in your style while your boss is autocratic, your boss may actually see you as subversive.

Here are some suggestions to help you lessen the threat or the suspicion:

Establish your competence. Just like the tax specialist, be indispensable. Be more knowledgeable, skilled, expert than others. Be careful not to be seen as withholding, as some mavericks are. That is, contribute your expertise as often as you can, so you broadcast the message that what you know and can do are completely at the service of the organization. Speak up often, suggest, and innovate. This mode of behavior is contrary to that of some competent mavericks who leave the impression that they are gearing themselves up to leave, to take their expertise elsewhere when they have developed it, thanks to the help of their present employer.

Produce. Keep the bottom line favorable. Your peers and bosses may not agree with your philosophy and methodology but if the results are right they can't help agreeing with the output. However, be advised that if you are perceived as being counterculture even high productivity may not save you. That's a compelling reason why you want to build your outside network for the day when you feel you have to leave—or are told to leave. Incidentally, your tenure in an alien culture may impress your next potential employer. A young acquaintance of mine went to a western state to head up a branch office for his company. He had to work closely with a successful, well-known distributor. Unfortunately the distributor was well-known also as extremely difficult to work with. It took time, but my young friend did forge a productive working relationship with this very difficult person. Later he left the company to take on a job in the area with a local corporation. His interviewer said to him, "If you could work with that so-and-so, you could get along anywhere."

Stay close to your boss. Don't appear to have any secrets. Let your boss know what your plans are, how your people are achieving, what you think could be improved. Your boss can't feel very suspicious or threatened if he or she knows almost every move you make.

Don't brag. This point has been made elsewhere in this book, but it is important enough to be repeated. When you describe what you have achieved, talk about the end product, the results. Yes, of course, you were exceptional in your ability to bring them about. But there's no point in antagonizing your boss by trumpeting your excellence. The results will speak for you.

Soft-pedal your disparate methods. This is another reason for concentrating on results and output. You don't want to continually remind your boss that your methods, so different from his or hers, work so well. When your boss advises you on what methods or techniques to use, listen respectfully. You don't have to tout your own "superior" approaches. When the boss achieves success using his or her ways, be gracious and praise the accomplishment.

Maintain close relationships with other managers. If you keep to yourself too much, you're broadcasting a message that you don't need or care for them. If you are friendly, open in your communications, and forthright and generous with your time, many of your peers will come to say, "He's different, and I don't agree with the way he does things, but he's a nice guy, and he gets results."

BRINGING CONFLICT INTO THE OPEN

Few people are comfortable with conflict. In fact, many people shut it off or suppress it. But since you are on the power track, coming up with ideas, competing for greater responsibility, searching for more resources to manage, you are bound to find yourself in conflict with others. It will happen, as long as you are trying to get things done and grab more for yourself. It will happen when others on whom you depend let you down, and you feel as if your reputation may be tarnished. It will happen when someone who dislikes you decides to do you in.

When you are out for more power, therefore, conflict is unavoidable. You must be skilled in dealing with it, otherwise you can lose ground, your power base can be eroded, you can lose friends and allies. If you know how to handle yourself in a conflict situation, you can come out stronger, looking like a hero, with increased visibility.

Much conflict is destructive. People let it get this

way. For example, conflict in many organizations with many people is characterized by the following:

It gets personal. The dispute usually starts over an issue or an idea, and it wasn't sufficiently resolved. The disputants shift their attention away from the issue that divided them and direct it to a personal level, perhaps suggesting the other is less than trustworthy, has dishonorable motives, is manipulative, etc. If you're in conflict with another who begins to spread untrue and scurrilous gossip, don't yield to the temptation to return the treatment. The only people who benefit from an ugly personal dispute are onlookers who aren't involved and who don't have to work closely with either of you. They enjoy the spectacle. Stay on the bedrock of solution finding, don't get mired in insults. If the name calling gets nasty on the other side, let people know you want to find a solution, that you find the other's behavior appalling and not helpful to the organization. This is a time to use the grapevine and your network of allies.

It leads to polarization. A fight that has gone on too long or become too fierce results in a polarization of people and issues. If you let this happen, you may force some of your allies to choose the other side because of loyalty, politics, or in return for past favors. When conflict becomes polarized, the combatants spend so much time explaining and defending their respective positions that they can't seem to move away from them. There is also pressure to save face.

To avoid this screaming across chasms, forget who did what to cause the problem. Be the first to come up with a solution that involves some concession—it needn't be great—on your part. Now you've put the other person on the defensive, because you've signaled that you are ready to negotiate. If the other person is acting in good faith, she will respond accordingly. You look like a hero acting in the best interests of the organiztion.

The main issues are lost. Sometimes a conflict drags on so long that no one is certain what started it. The original issue is no longer important. New issues are invented and old ones are reinvented to keep the fire smoldering. At this point the conflict has a momentum of its own. Don't get involved in trading laundry lists of complaints. Define the main issue and insist that it be solved before anything else is considered.

Because conflict is threatening to onlookers who might like to stay out of it but fear they can't, the hero in the organization is the one who takes the initiative and tries to resolve or at least manage the dispute. So when another department head is feuding with you on working relations between the departments, or someone is fighting your ideas, or some misunderstanding arises between you and another, be the first to suggest a solution. Or at least use the assertive-responsive approach: Here's the situation. Neither of us likes it. What can we do about it?

In most cases your steps to resolve the problem will work, for some of the following reasons:

1. The person on the other side of the conflict has a point of view that is just as legitimate to him or her as yours is to you. Don't belittle that point of view. It hardens the resistance and you may offend some power people who happen to agree with the other person.

2. The other person may also be uncomfortable about the conflict, but he doesn't know what to do about it. It's your move. If you want to increase the discomfort, step up the conflict. For example, he's opposing your idea to set up a new project. Start selling harder, line up wider support, if you can, and it will make the other person squirm. On the other hand, if you want the conflict resolved, move in quickly, show that you are in command and know exactly what you're doing. You'll look good as a result.

3. The other person is usually willing to accept a solution if you can make it sufficiently attractive. At least he or she can be persuaded to work with you to formulate a resolution of the conflict. If you make an offer and the other person refuses to consider it, others will tend to be exasperated with his stubbornness.

4. It is safer and wiser to keep to the issues in any discussion and avoid personal arguments. Be the cool one who keeps defining the issues in a rational manner. You gain points at the expense of your other combatant if he or she loses control and starts impugning your motives, your trustworthiness, or your general character. Others around you will tire of your opponent's childishness and venom. Meanwhile you stay above it, and stick to the issues.

5. The future is often a more constructive basis for discussion than the past. If the other person has a tail to pin on your donkey, wants to blame you, don't get into an endless yes-you-did, no-I-didn't discussion. Stay calm, and say, "That's in the past, now let's come up with a solution." It's very important that you not only

come up with a solution or an answer, but that you look as if you are always in control.

DEALING WITH AN ATTACK

You are walking down a corridor or sitting in a meeting. Suddenly one of your colleagues begins to berate you about something. It's an embarrassing situation because it takes place in public. The first thing you want to do is stop the attack, but remember that the other person is risking more. Most people don't care for scenes, and usually higher management places a premium on rationality.

You can opt to say nothing, hoping that the other person will run out of steam when you don't fight back. Don't reply in kind. That will put you on the same level and feed the fire. If you're in a group, get help. You might say, "I think this is a private matter to be discussed between Barbara and me. I don't think we should take up the group's time with this." Undoubtedly other members of the group will urge Barbara to cool off.

If you're in a hallway and the attack continues, walk away. If you can get a word in, say something such as, "This is not the appropriate place to discuss the subject. If you want to talk to me in private, call me in my office." Then turn your back on your attacker and walk away quickly. It's risky, because your walking away may inflame the other person more. But it's a better gamble than continuing to be yelled at, and you reduce the other person to a foolish position.

Perhaps the attack comes in the form of a memo. The most insidious memos are those that are clever and funny, yet savage. It's a touchy situation for you, because other people have probably seen the memo—or will see it. The initiative is your attacker's. Some suggestions:

Don't try to outdo the original memo in sarcasm and hostile humor. The response can't match the impact of the original. Also there are people who probably disapprove of putting that kind of thing in writing who'll be negative toward your response, too.

Discuss the memo and your planned response with your boss. First you want your boss to know that you're interested in resolving the conflict without impeding the organization's effectiveness. Second, you want to tap whatever good advice or helpful information he or she has to offer.

You and your boss may agree that you should not respond in any way. Your boss may be sufficiently upset that he or she wants to have a few words with the boss of the attacker. The issue can then be settled at a higher level, and probably not to the advantage of the person who wrote the memo. High level intervention can make you look very good. When I was a young man, I brashly got into a conflict with a senior, well-established and powerful colleague. Much to his surprise, two vice presidents, his boss and mine, intervened to settle the dispute. Needless to say, my elder colleague was tremendously impressed, and we had a mutually respectful relationship for the remaining time I worked with him.

But if the issue must be addressed:

Set up a meeting with the manager who sent the memo. Your attacker probably doesn't want a face-to-face meeting. That's probably why he or she resorted to writing the memo. But if you suggest getting together, your antagonist can hardly refuse. If you are reluctant to go to the other person's office, you can assume the other person would rather not come to yours. Suggest a quiet meeting in a conference room or someone else's temporarily vacant office.

When you meet, be controlled. Tell the other person, "We have a problem, and I'd like to see whether we can work it out." Don't make threats or suggest that the writing of the memo will have unpleasant consequences for the writer. He or she will probably feel compelled to adopt an I'm-not-afraid-of-you approach. You'll reach a standoff.

Stick with the issues. Listen to your colleague. You don't have to respond. Just give the other person every chance to air the grievance. If the person gets personal, remind him or her that you are there to deal with issues, not personalities. Stay in control, keep the conversation centered on solutions. You don't have to agree with his or her analysis of the situation, but you can say, "Okay, what would you rather see? or "What's a reasonable alternative?" If you don't agree, say so. Offer your suggestion. If you do agree, then you have the basis for a "contract."

Don't badmouth your attacker. There are people who will be most happy to let the writer of the memo know, and they'll be pleased to know that you are upset. Don't give them the opportunity or the satisfaction. You can say, "Yes, it was a very unfortunate memo." Or, "It's too bad she resorted to that." Those answers are ambiguous. Let it be known through the grapevine, or among your colleagues, that you have held a meeting to work things out. The contrast won't escape them: Your attacker took public, sneaky means to embarrass you; you took a mature, confident, private approach to settle things. If this approach doesn't settle things, or if you get another nasty memo, you want to take stronger action. You may take the issue to your boss and urge him or her to take the matter higher. Don't be hesitant to express that such memos are disruptive. They impede chances for constructive relations. They demoralize your subordinates and erode your power base. You might even want to mention that continuing to write such memos when you have taken steps to work things out in a *rational* way suggests a mental imbalance. Perhaps the issue should be aired in a four-way meeting involving you, your antagonist, and your respective bosses. Now is the time to call out the big guns. Make it everyone's issue.

MANAGING CONFLICT

Many people prefer to talk about conflict management rather than conflict resolution, if only because conflict will always be present in one form or another, especially if you are on the power track. Sometimes it takes the form of a rivalry with another, and if the relationship doesn't turn bitter and personal, it can actually have positive consequences. It will keep you sharp, knowing there is someone competing with you. Most constructive rivalries are more friendly than not. There is a little banter, ribbing, some power maneuvering, but the competitors work together. They keep their rivalry within the bounds of good manners and discretion, knowing that if their competition causes them to impede the efforts of the organization to achieve its goals, they could both lose out.

There are also personality conflicts. Some people don't like you, and probably never will. Again, even if you dislike a colleague, you can still work together. You may not enjoy the working relationship, but the alternative of refusing to be cooperative is self-defeating. You manage the conflict, keeping it within proper bounds.

There are some conflicts that are very minor, created by people who are not powerful enough to threaten you. For example, an old-timer well on the way to retirement raises a fuss about the way you tackle a project. Chances are no one is listening to him. He has long since lost his power base. You may want to ignore the complaints, continuing to treat him with respect. That's unwritten protocol. Don't waste your energy trying to placate people who have little or no power to do you harm.

Where there is potential for damage, move fast. Very often, the resolution of a serious conflict shows you to be skilled in your political expertise. People will admire the resolute, confident way you move quickly to restrict damage. Furthermore, if you move fairly as well as fast, you may turn an antagonist into an ally. It you don't move, you may leave your flank unprotected. As I've pointed out, prolonged conflict can injure you, erode management's interest in you, encourage them to think you may be a troublemaker.

Few people, relatively speaking, know how to manage conflict. If you want power, you want to be one of them. An essential part of managing conflict is knowing how to be a graceful winner. Some considerations:

Avoid destruction. When you bring power to bear on your opponent, use only what you need. Don't train the heavy artillery on a small patrol. When you display too much power, people become nervous about you. They fear the same thing might happen to them.

Give something up to the other person. If you can find something to concede, to help the other person save face, you avoid a total win-lose game.

Stop when you've won your goal. Don't use victory as an immediate stepping-stone to other requests or demands. You will have more strength later if you stop now, satisfied with what you've achieved. If you push too hard and too far, others may feel it necessary to band together to stop you. Don't risk losing the war.

Grace in victory is even more rare than grace in defeat, and it should be as highly respected. Indicate by your attitude that you are not smug or gloating about your triumph, and make specific moves of reconciliation to your opponent. Offer your cooperation and whatever other resources you have to make another's defeat easier to bear.

15

WHAT POWER LOOKS LIKE

Power is a state of mind. It is also an appearance, and it's equally true, that it's a manner of behavior.

People who would characterize themselves as assertive believe that they have a right to to try and satisfy their needs and wants. It doesn't mean, of course, that they have a right to get what they want or need, but they do have every right to try.

This is very true of power. If you want it, you have every right to seek it. You may not always get it, but if you don't seek it, you certainly won't get it. Seldom does power come to a person when it isn't sought.

Powerful people are positive. They have a positive mental attitude and they understand the power of positive thinking. Such slogans, labels, and trademarks may sound banal, but like all clichés, there is a core of truth. When you are in the company of positive people, you know it. They give off energy, and people around them get energized. That's one reason why positive people get more things done than negative people, especially when the doing involves other people. Energized people want to perform, to achieve, to satisfy.

True, there is the power of the veto, as I dealt with in a previous chapter, but it is a short term and limited power. People who go through life saying "no" are very poor in running an organization. In effect, they run a closed system, with high barriers and restricted output. They try to maintain a status quo while the environment changes. Maintenance in management is a regressive function.

Positive powerful people, on the other hand, are open systems. They have boundaries to protect themselves from simply being invaded and run over by others and outside forces. These boundaries do not prohibit them from being aware that times and conditions change, that new forces are operative, that resources must be shaped and developed to meet the different challenges. Positive powerful people are receptive, sensitive, and adaptive. They see change as a potential opportunity, not a threat. They are, as has been pointed out, "what if . . . ?" people.

Most people in a gathering will be drawn to positive powerful people as if to a magnet. There is an energy field around them. This is not to say that positive powerful people are necessarily attractive personalities. Some who have made it to the top, have become wealthy and influential, can be crude, amoral or even immoral, cruel, abrasive, and unpleasant in myriad ways. But in a crowd they do not go unnoticed or ignored.

It has been a thesis of this book that you do not

have to be amoral or immoral, nasty or crude to gain power, quite the contrary. You can go after power and still retain the respect of everyone around you. In fact, that's a more secure base for your power. If people respect you, they will work with you. If they do not respect you, or trust you, they will work against you, at least covertly. On the other hand, liking you probably has little or nothing to do with how people feel about cooperating and collaborating with you. It's doubtful that many people will like you when you acquire power. You're showing them up when you do. You are providing them with a contrast that is uncomfortable for them.

If you are successful, they will work with you, be your allies, support you. You have proved yourself a winner, and generally speaking people like to be associated with a winner.

THE APPEARANCE OF POWER

There is such a thing as a power image. You have to work to create it. Your clothes are one example. When I was a young editor, I set out to break the dress code in my company. In the summer I came to work with no jacket or tie. In the winter I wore turtle neck sweaters with sports jackets. There was a lot of talk and some grumbling, and I had to take a fair amount of hostile humor. In time, others began to relax in their dress. A colleague then said to me chidingly, "You are a managing editor. You have written books. You are considered an authority on management. You ought to dress like one." She was right, and while others around me were enjoying a liberalized informal dress code, I went back to wearing three-piece suits. I could immediately detect increased respect.

I advocate more formality in your dress when you want to create an image of power. Even though many of your meetings may be shirt-sleeve affairs, you should consider retaining some formality. It sets you apart. In fact, I will go further to suggest that you have as your goal being one of the better-dressed people in your organization. Not only does it help your image, being well-dressed also helps your self-confidence. When you dress attractively, people will take you more seriously, and you, interestingly, will take yourself more seriously.

Look around you. One of your colleagues has a wrinkled, somewhat old-looking shirt; it doesn't appear quite clean. Another wears a suit that seldom looks pressed; the pants are baggy, there's a slight rip in the back of his vest that he seems not to care about. Still another wears strange colored pants and jackets that don't quite go together. How do you feel when you look at them?

Some time ago I attended an awards ceremony sponsored by a very large professional association. It was an elaborate dinner in a very elegant hotel. The guest of honor was a former president of the association, a man known throughout the industry, an author of books. When the award was announced, the man came up to the podium wearing a sports jacket and slacks. I felt as if the man's reputation and achievements did not exist. The man's image and appearance spoke deafeningly.

When you look around at your colleagues who dress in poor taste, are ill groomed or sloppy, you probably have a sense of superiority. That's how others probably feel about you, too, that you have a quality that the others do not have, that you are to be taken more seriously.

YOUR COMMUNICATING

Nothing damages the appearance of power than poor speaking skills. Time after time I've sat listening to powerful people, such as CEOs of large corporations, give dreary, dull, unimaginative and unimpressive talks. Well, they've made it to the top, so perhaps they can afford to look bad, but chances are, you haven't made it to the top. You are well advised to think about how you communicate. Work on your writing and speaking. I've already suggested that you invest in a public speaking course or workshop. It is money well invested.

Writing is different. It takes a long time to develop good writing skills. It takes lots of practice, but when you do it well, people will pay attention to you. They will read what you write, and accord you more credibility than someone who writes with less skill. I cannot, in this last chapter, impart the writing expertise that will help you in your search for greater power. I can however give you some standards for which you can aim.

First, good writing is good thinking; clear writing is clear thinking. If you have it straight in your head and try to get it on paper just that way, you have a better chance of being considered a good and clear writer. Much muddy writing, especially by professionals and academicians, often passes for profound thinking. It may be, but very often it is muddled thinking. Some of the most profound thinking emerges as clear, simple words on paper. When I did graduate work in philosophy, even though my French was primitive, I found it possible to read some of the modern French philosophers in their native language. That is good and clear writing.

Second, the writing that will have the greatest impact on others sounds the way you talk. That's right, the closer you can get in your writing style to your manner of speaking, the better you will look on paper. So get in the habit of reading aloud what you write. Train yourself to ask, as you read, "Do I sound that way?"

Both in writing and in speaking, you cannot lose if you take time to think before you express yourself. When you have it clear in your head what you want to say, you will be much more influential. For some as yet unknown reason, people who speak at a fairly rapid pace carry more credibility than those who speak slowly, according to psychological research. The more thinking you do before opening your mouth, the better your chance of speaking confidently, clearly, and at a brisk pace. It also helps if you speak in a lower register. People who have high pitched voices undermine their seriousness. Train yourself to lower your voice. People tend to give more attention to baritones than tenors. Concentrate on putting whole sentences together. If you stumble, hesitate, back up, you will convey a poor image, lack of self-confidence, and indecisiveness.

In meetings, be sure to make *substantial* contributions. In far too many of the thousands of meetings I've attended over the years, I've listened to people who obviously thought they were enhancing their image by simply paraphrasing or parroting what had already been said. They gained, instead, the contempt of their colleagues. If you wish to support what someone has already said, do so, but don't delude yourself that you can repeat it in different words and score points. If you have something original to say only once in a while, you will be remembered for that.

SUSPICIOUS BEHAVIORS

Occasionally you will walk into an office and be invited to sit in a chair that puts you lower than the person behind the desk. This is a power move, you are being placed at a disadvantage. People who are alert and sophisticated laugh at such clumsiness and transparency. In this situation, my advice is to either sit comfortably or stand against the wall, preferably so that you tower over the seated person. In time you'll probably force him or her to stand, equalizing your situations.

The same advice applies to that other transparent trick, forcing you to sit facing the sun. Just say, "I'm sorry, the sun is in my eyes. Do you mind if I move the chair?" The other person is counting on your not noticing or being too intimidated to do anything about it.

I've met some people who thought that one way to be perceived as being on the power track is to always be in a hurry. The man who was probably one of the least competent managers I ever knew followed this pattern. He was always rushing, but it didn't take his colleagues and subordinates long to realize that once he got where he was headed, he didn't do anything. I generally advise people to avoid transparent devices such as this. Besides, if you walk more slowly, you'll see and hear more. People will want to talk with you. That's how you keep abreast of what is going on.

NEGOTIATING YOUR POWER

People who get where they want to go usually get there because they never lose sight of their destination. If your superordinate goal is to go as far as you can in the organization and garner as much power as you can, then you don't let yourself be sidetracked by conflict, petty power games, and competition that has short-range satisfaction. Nor are you advised to be a jungle fighter, making your way over the corpses of people who worked with you. Being crude, amoral, or immoral, insensitive, believing in the survival of the fittest, will work for a time. It's almost axiomatic, however, that jungle fighters have to change jungles regularly. Even then, their reputation often precedes them, and there are groups of "natives" already waiting to ambush them.

If you want to build a power base that is secure and long-lasting, reject the image of the power-talker who cheats, lies, manipulates, steals and intimidates. It may make good novels and television drama, but is unsuccessful in the real organizational world.

Most power, in fact, is negotiated. There is just so much power to be divided between the people who want it, including you. Some will come to you almost automatically, as I've discussed, because of your position, your competence and your associations. The rest you must seek. When you add to your power, it means that others have given up some of theirs. You will find that some of the people you work with can be persuaded to do just that. Your boss is an example. When it makes him or her look good by giving you more space, authority, responsibility and power, your boss becomes a significant collaborator in your power-building. As I've pointed out, your subordinates can also greatly help you by enhancing your image of competence and success. Some of your peers will also become part of your power base when they see that by doing so they can achieve some of their own agendas; by teaming up with you, they can gain more influence, esteem, and success by association.

Others in the organization may not want to resist you, but they will not necessarily be moved to contribute to your progress on the power track. Your hope may be that they stay out of your way. And they will probably do that, provided that they don't see harm coming their way from you or that you won't deprive them of their security. There are times when you will want to respect the neutrals. If your manner is not vindictive or otherwise threatening, you will avoid arousing the fears and anxieties of such coworkers.

For those who want to resist you or compete with you, your course is clear. You may often have to negotiate contracts with them, person by person. There are times when it even will be in their interest to join with you or to collaborate with you, but you will have to show them the advantage. With these people, you build your power base block. It's a painstaking process. But if you are in control of yourself, know where you are heading, are more sensitive than they are to what is going on, know where the power centers are, what the power dynamics are, and draw from every source of power you can on a continuing basis, you have a good chance of winning over them. Some of your would-be competitors will simply give up. The realities of your superior power position will be clear. And when you've won, be a gracious winner.

It's important to remember that power contracts are seldom in perpetuity. People make them with you to fulfill their own objectives, whatever those objectives may be. When fulfillment occurs, the other party may consider the contract to have been completed. So you will have to be ever on the alert to find new contracts to make, or to renew old ones. Don't take your allies for granted, or misuse their loyalty to you. Know what they want, and, if it is in your power, help them to get what they want.

If you become widely known as a person who is open to making contracts and one who keeps them, you'll find it easier, as time passes, to sell yourself and the idea of joining with you. You'll become more influential and powerful as people say to themselves and among themselves, "You can do 'business' with him (or her)."

You need to be congruent. That doesn't mean that you have to tell everyone exactly what you want or what your objectives are. But it is important that you do not say one thing and do the opposite. Silence is much more preferable than deception. You want to be a straight-shooter. Remember, the people who give you power can also find ways of taking it away from you.

INDEX